Book brie

1 *The Valley of Fear* is the fourth a
Holmes novel by British writer
Conan Doyle. The story was first published in
Strand Magazine in 1914.

2 The novel is written in two parts: in the first
part, Dr Watson, as narrator, describes how
Sherlock Holmes solves a murder in an English
country manor. In the second part, there is the
story behind the mystery and the explanation
of past events.

3 The second part of the book is loosely based
on the Molly Maguires, an Irish and American
crime organisation, and is used to comment on
the politics and union problems in Ireland and
America at that time.

4 Sherlock Holmes only appears in the first part
and in the epilogue at the end of the second
part of the novel.

5 *The Valley of Fear* is one of the Sherlock Holmes
novels completed after Conan Doyle tried to kill
him off - along with his mortal enemy Professor
Moriarty - in The Final Problem.

In this reader:

21st Century Skills
To encourage students to connect the story to the world they live in.

B2 FIRST
B2 level activities.

Culture Notes
Brief cultural information.

Glossary
An explanation of difficult words.

Picture Caption
A brief explanation of the picture.

Audio
These icons indicate the parts of the story that are recorded:
start ▶ stop ■

Sir Arthur Conan Doyle

The Valley of Fear

Adaptation and Activities by
Pauline Russo

Illustrated by
Claudio Scaramuzzi

Young Adult (ELI) **Readers**

Young Adult Eli Readers

The **ELI Readers** collection is a complete range of books and plays for readers of all ages, ranging from captivating contemporary stories to timeless classics. There are four series, each catering for a different age group: **First ELI Readers**, **Young ELI Readers**, **Teen ELI Readers** and **Young Adult ELI Readers**. The books are carefully edited and beautifully illustrated to capture the essence of the stories and plots. The readers are supplemented with 'Focus on' texts packed with background cultural information about the writers and their lives and times.

The Valley of Fear
Sir Arthur Conan Doyle
Retold and activities by
Pauline Russo

Illustrations
Claudio Scaramuzzi

**ELI Readers
Founder and Series Editors**
*Paola Accattoli, Grazia Ancillani,
Daniele Garbuglia (Art Director)*

Graphic Design
Emilia Coari

Production Manager
Francesco Capitano

Photo credits
Shutterstock

© 2025
**Gruppo editoriale ELi
P.O. Box 6
62019 Recanati (MC)
Italy
T** +39 071750701
F +39 071977851
**info@elionline.com
www.elionline.com**

*Typeset in 10,5 / 15 pt Monotype Fulmar
Printed in Italy by Tecnostampa –
Pigini Group Printing Division
Loreto – Trevi (Italia) – ERA 427.10*

**ISBN 978-88-536-4585-2
www.eligradedreaders.com**

Contents

Sherlock Holmes
The great
London detective

Dr John Watson
Holmes' assistant and
narrator of the story

Inspector Alec MacDonald
An Inspector from
Scotland Yard

White Mason
The police detective
from Birlstone

Cecil Barker
John Douglas's friend
and ex business partner

Mrs Douglas
John Douglas's
wife

Mr Douglas
The owner of
Birlstone Manor

PART 2

Jack McMurdo
The protagonist
in part 2

Ettie Shafter
Jack McMurdo's
girlfriend

Jacob Shafter
Owner of the boarding
house and Ettie's father

Bodymaster John McGinty
Head of the Vermissa Lodge
and the Scowrers

Ted Baldwin
A Scowrer

Morris
A member of the
Vermissa Lodge

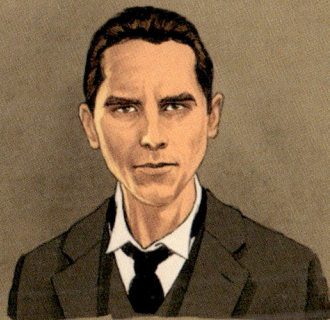

Mike Scanlan
A lodge member and
McMurdo's friend

Grammar

1 **Fill the gaps with the correct preposition A, B, C or D.**

This story **(1)** .... Sir Arthur Conan Doyle is a classic Sherlock Holmes mystery, narrated **(2)** .... Dr Watson. It starts **(3)** .... the murder of a rich man called John Douglas, in a country house **(4)** .... Sussex, England. Inspector MacDonald, from Scotland Yard, visits Holmes at his London apartment and asks him for help **(5)** .... this difficult case. Holmes and Dr Watson go immediately with him **(6)** .... the scene of the crime. It's a complicated case but, with his usual intelligence, Holmes manages to solve the mystery. This all takes place **(7)** .... the first part of the novel. The second part takes place in the past and gives more details **(8)** .... the reasons for the murder.

1	**A** with	**B** by	**C** about	**D** for
2	**A** by	**B** at	**C** about	**D** from
3	**A** on	**B** about	**C** for	**D** with
4	**A** from	**B** at	**C** in	**D** of
5	**A** at	**B** to	**C** of	**D** with
6	**A** on	**B** for	**C** to	**D** at
7	**A** on	**B** in	**C** about	**D** at
8	**A** for	**B** about	**C** in	**D** with

Vocabulary

2 **Make adjectives from the following nouns.**

1 guilt   ....
2 confidence   ....
3 amazement   ....
4 respect   ....
5 suspicion   ....
6 value   ....

Crossword

3 **Complete the crossword, then read Chapter 1 and check your answers.**

Clues

1 Part of a chain; a connection
2 Opposite of innocent
3 Code used to solve a puzzle
4 Another name for a criminal
5 An illegal act
6 Sure about something
7 To say something bad about someone or something
8 To steal something from a person or place
9 One of many publications of the same book
10 Very surprised

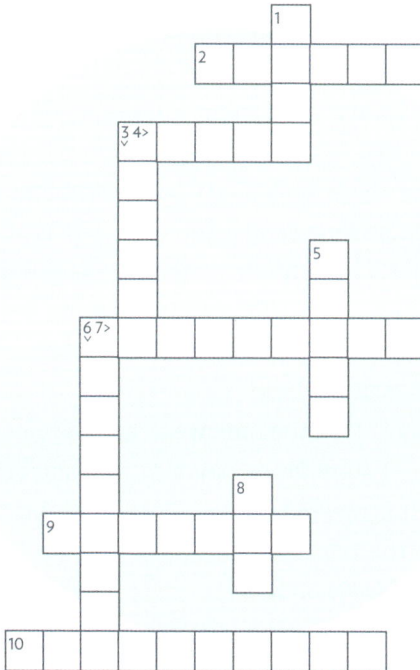

PART 1:
THE TRAGEDY OF BIRLSTONE

Chapter 1

The Warning

▶ 2 Sherlock Holmes sat at the breakfast table, studying a letter.

'It's Porlock's writing,' he said thoughtfully. 'So, it will be something very important.'

'Who is Porlock?' I asked.

'It's a false name, Watson. I don't know him, but he is not important – it's who he knows that's important. Have you heard of Professor Moriarty?'

'Yes, he's a criminal who is famous among crooks*, but unknown to the public.'

'In the eyes of the law, Moriarty isn't a criminal. He's a genius but a devil. However, he's never suspected or criticised. After all, he's the famous mathematician who wrote the excellent book 'The Dynamics of an Asteroid'. But I'm sure I'll get him one day.'

'That's something I want to see!' I exclaimed. 'But you were speaking of this man Porlock.'

'Ah yes, Porlock. He's the only weak link* I've been able to find in Moriarty's chain. I sometimes pay him for valuable information. I'll be able to read this message once I have the cipher*.'

Holmes put the paper on the table and we both looked at the strange coded message on it.

'I' refers to Dr Watson, the narrator of the story.

Prof. Moriarty is a criminal mastermind and Sherlock's arch enemy*. He uses his intelligence to help other criminals but never gets caught. Conan Doyle based his character on a real-life criminal called Adam Worth.

---

crook a criminal
arch enemy greatest/main enemy

link part of a chain, a connection
cipher a secret message, code

534 C2 13 127 36 31 4 17 21 41
DOUGLAS 109 293 5 37 BIRLSTONE
26 BIRLSTONE 9 47 171

'It's clearly a reference to words on the pages of some book. I can do nothing till I know which book and which page.'

'But why are there the names 'Douglas' and 'Birlstone'?'

'Clearly because these words are not on the page of the book.'

'Then why has he not given the name of the book?'

'My dear Watson, it's better not to put the cipher and the message in the same envelope. Another letter will arrive soon with an explanation, and the name of the book.'

Holmes was right. A few minutes later, another letter with the same writing on it arrived, and this time it was signed. But when he read it, he said, 'Dear me, Watson! I hope that the man Porlock won't be in danger.'

'DEAR MR HOLMES (he says):

I will go no further in this matter. It is too dangerous. I can see that he suspects me. He came to me after I had addressed this envelope to you. He didn't see it but I saw he was suspicious*. Please burn the other message, which can now be of no use to you.

FRED PORLOCK.'

suspicious showing no trust

Holmes sat with the letter in his hand. At last, he said:

'Perhaps he just feels guilty and that's why he saw suspicion in the other's eyes.'

'The other being, I suppose, Professor Moriarty.'

'Of course. Porlock is clearly very afraid. I can see this from the writing on the second envelope.'

'So, why did he write a second letter at all?'

'Because he knew I wouldn't forget the first one and that could cause problems for him.'

'Of course,' I said, and I picked up the original coded message. 'I can't believe that there may be an important secret on this paper, and we can't read it.'

'Let's think about this,' said Sherlock. 'The message begins with a large number, 534. So, if that is a page number, that means it's a large book. The next sign is C2. What do you think of that, Watson?'

'The second chapter, no doubt.'

'That can't be it, Watson. You'll agree, I'm sure, that if the page number is given, the number of the chapter isn't necessary. Also, if page 534 is only in the second chapter, the first one would have to be very long.'

'Column!' I cried.

'Brilliant, Watson. So now, you see, it must be a large book printed in long double columns, since one of the words is number 293. He was going to send me the clue to the book in his second letter, so it must be a very common book, which he imagines I would already have.'

'The Bible!' I cried.

Dr Watson is a loyal friend. Holmes admires him and often asks for his help with his cases. He's a medical doctor and an intelligent man, but he doesn't have the same talent that Holmes has for solving puzzles.

Holmes and Watson read the secret message.

'Good, Watson, good! But not, if I may say so, quite good enough! There are many editions of the Bible, I don't think they would have the same page numbers. For the same reason, it can't be the dictionary. So what else?'

'An almanac!'

'Excellent, Watson! Whitaker's Almanac is in common use and has many pages with double columns.'

An almanac is a book that is published annually, containing useful information, for the current year.

Holmes took the book from his desk and told me to write down the words that the coded message referred to. Afterwards, I looked at the strange message which said:

"There - is - danger -may - come - very - soon - one Douglas - rich - country - now - at - Birlstone - House - Birlstone - confidence - is - pressing"

'What a strange way of showing what he means to say!' I said.

'On the contrary*, he has done very well,' said Holmes. 'It's difficult to find the words you want in the columns and you have to depend on the intelligence of the reader. It's perfectly clear. Something bad is going to happen to someone called Douglas, a rich country gentleman. He's written 'confidence' but I'm sure he means he's confident that it's pressing*.'

Scotland Yard, which also refers to the Metropolitan Police Force, is the London police headquarters.

Holmes was still enjoying his success when the door opened, and Inspector MacDonald of Scotland Yard came into the room. Those were the early days at the end of the 1880s, when Alec MacDonald was not yet famous, but still a young police detective. He liked and respected Holmes, and asked him for help with difficult cases.

on the contrary in contrast (the opposite)

pressing urgent

Holmes didn't have many friends but he liked the Scotsman, and smiled when he saw him.

'You're up early, Mr Mac,' said Holmes. 'I fear that means that something bad has happened.'

'Knowing you well, I suppose you mean 'hope' not 'fear', Mr Holmes,' the inspector answered with a smile. Then he looked at the table, in amazement, and saw the secret message.

'Douglas!' he said with surprise. 'Birlstone! What's this, Mr Holmes? Where on earth did you get those names?'

'It's a cipher Dr Watson and I had to solve. But why – what's wrong with those names?'

The inspector looked at both of us in astonishment and said, 'Mr Douglas of Birlstone Manor House was murdered last night!'

My friend, Sherlock, loved these dramatic moments but showed no emotion.

'You don't seem surprised,' said the inspector.

'Interested, Mr Mac, but not really surprised. I received an important letter warning me that a certain person is in danger. Now I learn that he's dead. I'm interested but, as you can see, not surprised.'

Holmes told him about Porlock and the letters.

'I was going to ask you and Dr Watson to come to Birlstone with me this morning,' explained the inspector. 'But perhaps it would be better to find this man Porlock.'

MacDonald examined the envelope containing the coded message.

'Posted in London - that doesn't help us much. You say Porlock is a false name, and that you sometimes send him money to a post office box. Have you ever gone to see who comes to get it?'

'On earth' added to what, where, when, how or why questions, gives emphasis and expresses surprise or disbelief.

Holmes is well-known for showing very little excitement, even when he is pleased about something.

People pay for a box at the post office, where they receive mail when they don't want the sender to know their address.

'No,' said Holmes. 'because I promised not to look for him. I know there's another person behind him.'

'This professor you often talk about?'

'Exactly!'

Inspector MacDonald smiled and looked quickly at me.

'I must say, Mr Holmes, that at Scotland Yard, we think you're wrong about this professor. He seems very respectable and intelligent. I, myself, went to talk to him.'

Holmes laughed and said, 'Great! Tell me, did you speak to the professor in his study?'

'Yes, I sat in front of his writing desk.'

'Did you notice a picture above the professor's head?'

'Yes, I saw the picture – a young woman with her head on her hands, looking to the side.'

'That painting is worth more than forty thousand pounds and, may I remind you,' said Holmes. 'that the professor's salary* is about seven hundred pounds a year.'

'Do you mean that he also earns his money illegally? That's amazing!' said the inspector.

'I'll tell you some things about Moriarty,' continued Holmes. 'He employs about a hundred different types of criminals, and he has many bank accounts, mostly in banks abroad.'

'That's very interesting, Holmes. But what is the connection between the professor and Birlstone, except for the warning from this man Porlock?'

The police never suspect Prof. Moriarty of any wrong-doing.

salary money earned for work

'There may be two motives*. First, this man Douglas may have done something to Moriarty, and the others have been told about his death so that they'll be too afraid to do the same. The other is that Moriarty organised the death of Mr Douglas for financial gain*. Was there also a robbery?'

'I haven't heard,' confirmed the inspector. 'We must go to Birlstone immediately then. I'll tell you and Dr Watson everything on the way there.' ■

---

motive reason for doing something   **gain** benefit

Reading

1 **Decide if the following sentences are True (T) or False (F).**

		T	F
1	Sherlock showed the letter to Dr Watson in the evening.	☐	☐
2	Sherlock knew who had sent him the letter.	☐	☐
3	Porlock's boss is Prof. Moriarty.	☐	☐
4	Porlock sent Sherlock the cipher in the second letter.	☐	☐
5	The Inspector wasn't surprised to see Douglas's name in the message.	☐	☐
6	The letter was posted in Birlstone.	☐	☐
7	Inspector MacDonald knows that Prof. Moriarty is a criminal.	☐	☐
8	The Inspector didn't know if there had also been a robbery.	☐	☐

Grammar   B2 FIRST

2 **Complete the text with one word for each space.**

Sherlock Holmes and Dr Watson **(1)** .... studying the letter when Inspector MacDonald arrived. He was a young Scotland Yard detective **(2)** .... often asked Holmes' help with his difficult **(3)** .... Holmes liked the young Scotsman and smiled **(4)** .... him. When the inspector saw the cipher they were looking **(5)** .... , he was shocked to see the names Douglas and Birlstone and asked **(6)** .... they had got the message from. Then, he told them that Mr Douglas **(7)** .... been murdered the night **(8)** ....

Holmes showed no emotion and said he was not surprised at **(9)** .... They decided to go to Birlstone together and the inspector would give Holmes and Watson all the details **(10)** .... the way.

Grammar

3 **Change the sentences from Direct to Indirect Speech.**

1 "Who is Porlock?" asked Dr Watson.

....

2 "He's the only weak link I've been able to find in Moriarty's chain," replied Holmes.

....

3 "I think you're wrong about Prof. Moriarty," said the Inspector to Holmes.

....

4 "What is the connection between the professor and Birlstone?" asked the Inspector.

....

5 "Was there also a robbery?" asked Holmes.

....

Pre-Reading Activities • PART 1: Chapter 2

Listening

▶ 3 **4** **Listen to the start of Chapter 2 and write a description and some facts about the main characters next to their picture.**

1
....
....
....

2
....
....
....

3
....
....
....

Chapter 2

The Facts of the Case

▶ 3 Before I describe other details of the tragic events of the night of January 6th, I'll describe the place and people involved in this mystery.

The ancient Manor House was close to the village of Birlstone in the county of Sussex. Part of the house was very old and dated back to the 11th century. It was surrounded by a moat, so the only way to get into the house was across a drawbridge*, which was raised every night and lowered every morning. This fact was very important.

Douglas was a strong man of about 50, and friendly to everyone. He had lots of money, which he had earned in the gold fields in California where he'd lived for many years before coming to Birlstone five years ago. His wife was a beautiful English lady, twenty years younger than her husband, whom she'd met in London when he was a widower*. Some people thought that perhaps she didn't know everything about her husband's past, and noticed she was very nervous when her husband came home late.

Another character in this mystery was Cecil Barker from London, a frequent and welcome visitor at the Manor House. He was present on the night John Douglas was killed. He'd met Douglas when he, too, was living in America, and was the only person who knew about

Birlstone is not the name of a real village in England. It was invented by Arthur Conan Doyle.

A moat was a channel of water built around a house or castle to protect it.

drawbridge a bridge that is raised to stop people crossing water to enter a building

widower a man whose wife has died

his past. Barker was also rich but unmarried, and at least five years younger than Douglas. He was a tall, broad man who was easy-going, but had the look of a boxer. He was very friendly with both Douglas and his wife, but sometimes the servants noticed that Douglas was irritated by Barker's friendship with his wife.

There were six servants in the house, plus Ames the butler*, and Mrs Allen, the housekeeper*.

Now, I'll explain what happened on January 6th. At 11.45pm, Cecil Barker rang the bell at the local police station to tell them that John Douglas had been murdered. Sergeant Wilson hurried back to the house with Mr Barker and found the drawbridge down and all the lights on. The butler and the servants were together in the hall, looking white and afraid. Only Mr Barker seemed calm. Just then, the doctor from the village, Dr Wood, arrived, and he entered the room where the tragedy had occurred, followed by the sergeant and Mr Barker. The butler quickly closed the door behind them to hide the horrible scene from the terrified servants.

The dead man was lying on his back in the centre of the room, with his arms and legs stretched out. He was wearing a dressing gown* over his night clothes, and slippers on his feet. The doctor held the table lamp over him and saw that a sawn-off shotgun* was lying across his chest. It was clear that he'd been shot in the face at close range*.

The country policeman was a little worried about the great responsibility which had come so suddenly upon him.

'We will touch nothing until my superiors arrive,' he said in a quiet voice, staring at the horrible sight before him.

---

butler head servant in a house who organises the other staff
housekeeper servant who organises the cooking and cleaning in another person's house

dressing gown a long robe worn over pyjamas
sawn-off shotgun an American rifle with the end cut off
at close range from a short distance

'Nothing has been touched up to now. I'm sure of that. This is exactly how I found him,' explained Mr Barker.

'When was that?' said the sergeant, taking out his notebook.

'It was just half past eleven. I was sitting by the fire in my bedroom when I heard a noise. I ran downstairs immediately.'

'Was the door open?'

'Yes, it was open,' replied Mr Barker.

'Poor Douglas was lying as you see him. His bedroom candle was burning on the table. I lit the lamp a few minutes later.'

'Did you see anyone?'

'No. I heard Mrs Douglas coming downstairs and I ran out to stop her from seeing this terrible sight. Mrs Allen came and took her away. Ames arrived and we went into the room together again.'

'I've heard that the drawbridge is kept up all night,' said the sergeant.

'Yes, it was up until I lowered it,' confirmed Barker.

'So, no one could have escaped. Mr Douglas must have shot himself then!'

'That was our first idea, but look at this!' Barker pulled open the curtain. The window was open wide. On the window sill* there was some blood with a boot print* in it. Do you see? Someone stood there while going out of the window. '

'You mean that someone waded across the moat to escape?'

'Exactly!'

'Then, if you came into the room immediately after the crime had been committed, that means he was in the water at that time.'

In Victorian times, houses did not have electricity. They used candles for moving from one room to another and oil lamps when they needed more light or light in a room for a longer time.

The moat was not very deep and it was possible for someone to walk through the water to the other side.

sill shelf under a window
boot print a mark left by a boot

Barker shows Sergeant Wilson the mark on the window sill.

'I have no doubt,' confirmed Mr Barker. 'I should have gone to the window but, with the curtain closed, I didn't think of it. And then I heard Mrs Douglas coming and I had to stop her from entering the room and seeing this horrible sight.'

'But then how did they get into the house if the drawbridge was up?' asked the sergeant. 'At what time was it raised?'

'Just before six o'clock,' said Ames, the butler. 'It's usually raised at half past four, but Mrs Douglas had visitors and I had to wait until they'd left. Then I raised it myself.'

'Then, the answer has to be this,' said Sergeant Wilson. 'Someone came across the bridge before six and hid until Mr Douglas came into the room after eleven o'clock. Then he escaped through the window, leaving his gun behind him.'

The sergeant picked up a card which lay on the floor. The initials V.V. and the number 341 were written on it.

'I don't know what that is,' said Barker. 'The murderer probably left it.'

Dr Wood noticed a large hammer lying in front of the fireplace. Cecil Barker explained that he'd seen Mr Douglas using it the day before to put up a picture. Sergeant Wilson took the lamp and looked around the room, then he pulled the curtain back again.

'Someone was definitely hiding here.' He held down the light and saw the marks of muddy boots in the corner. 'It looks like the man got into the house after the curtains were closed and before six when the bridge was raised. This is probably the first room he found, and he hid behind this curtain. He had probably wanted to burgle* the house but when Mr Douglas found him, he killed him and escaped.'

burgle to steal things from a house

Just then, the doctor noticed a mark on the dead man's right forearm*. It was a strange brown design, a triangle inside a circle. It was not a tattoo. The symbol had been burnt on to the man's skin.

'What's this mark?' he asked. 'Could this have any connection with the crime?'

'I don't know what it means,' said Cecil Barker, 'but I have seen the mark on Douglas many times in the last ten years.'

'And so have I,' said the butler. Suddenly he cried out and pointed at the dead man's hand.

'They've taken his wedding ring!' he gasped*. 'Mr Douglas always wore his plain gold wedding ring on the little finger of his left hand. That ring with the nugget was above it, and the snake ring was on the third finger. The other rings are there, but the wedding ring has gone.'

'That means the murderer took off the nugget ring to take the wedding ring and then put the nugget ring back again,' said the sergeant, shaking his head. 'White Mason is a smart man but I think we'll need help from London for this difficult case.'

Men often wore a ring with a rough piece of gold on it. Mr Douglas made his money in the gold mines in California.

When Holmes and I arrived at Birlstone station with Inspector MacDonald, White Mason was waiting to welcome us. He was a quiet but friendly person with a red face and a stout* body. In his tweed* suit, he looked like a small farmer or a retired gamekeeper*. He certainly didn't look like a country policeman. He took us to the village inn*, where he'd booked a room for us. He quickly told us all the facts that I described previously.

'Amazing!' said Holmes. 'Really amazing! I can't remember a case as strange as this.'

---

forearm the part of your arm from your wrist to your elbow
gasp to breathe in loudly and suddenly when shocked
stout quite fat

tweed rough woollen cloth
gamekeeper a person who takes care of wildlife
inn a pub where you can eat and sleep

'I thought you'd say that, Mr Holmes,' said White Mason in delight. 'When I met Sergeant Wilson at the house, I checked all the facts. I examined the hammer but there was no sign that Mr Douglas had used it to defend himself. The gun was less than two feet long and could easily have been carried under a man's coat. The letters P-E-N were on the gun but the rest of the name had been cut off when it was sawn*.'

A foot is a measurement of length used in the UK and US. One foot = 30.48 cm.

'Pennsylvania Small Arms Company – a well-known American firm,' said Holmes.

'No doubt it is an American shotgun,' White Mason continued. 'I've read that a sawn-off shotgun is used in some parts of America. So, that means that the man who entered the house and killed Mr Douglas was an American.'

Shotgun is the American word for a rifle. A sawn-off shotgun is associated with organised crime. The barrels were cut off the end of the rifle to make it shorter and easier to hide under a coat. It also made it easier to use at close range.

'But I've heard no evidence yet that any stranger was ever in the house,' said MacDonald, shaking his head.

'The open window, the blood on the window sill, the strange card, the marks of boots in the corner, the gun!' said White Mason.

'Nothing there that could not have been arranged. Mr Douglas was an American, or at least had lived in America. And Mr Barker too,' continued MacDonald.

'But Ames, the butler, has never seen a gun like that in the house,' protested White Mason.

'The ring and the card seem to show a personal and premeditated* act,' said MacDonald, shaking his stubborn* Scottish head. 'The man is not a burglar*, if there ever was one. He knew it would be difficult

sawn cut with a saw
premeditated planned

stubborn determined and not willing to change one's opinion.
burglar thief, robber

to leave the house, as it's surrounded by water. It would have made more sense to bring a silent weapon* to use, but he brought a noisy weapon that everyone could hear. What do you think, Mr Holmes?'

'You certainly present a strong case,' Holmes replied. 'Can we go to the house at once?'

'Of course, Mr Holmes. We are honoured by your presence, and you too Dr Watson,' said White Mason.

---

weapon something, like a knife or gun, used to harm another person.

Reading

1 **Read Chapter 2 again and choose the correct answer A, B or C.**

1 The Manor House was surrounded by...
☐ **A** a wood. ☐ **B** bushes. ☐ **C** a moat.

2 When Mrs Douglas met her husband, he was...
☐ **A** divorced. ☐ **B** a widower. ☐ **C** unmarried.

3 When John Douglas was found murdered, Cecil Barker...
☐ **A** called the police. ☐ **B** ran to the police station.
☐ **C** sent Ames to the police station.

4 Cecil Barker told the police that when he heard the noise, he was...
☐ **A** in the kitchen. ☐ **B** in his bedroom. ☐ **C** on the stairs.

5 When he went into the study, Barker...
☐ **A** opened the window. ☐ **B** lit a candle.
☐ **C** lit an oil lamp.

6 The mark on the dead man's arm was...
☐ **A** a circle with a triangle in it. ☐ **B** a triangle with a circle in it.
☐ **C** a triangle on top of a circle.

7 The murderer had taken Mr Douglas's ring that...
☐ **A** was like a snake. ☐ **B** had a nugget on it.
☐ **C** he'd got when he was married.

8 White Mason was...
☐ **A** a policeman. ☐ **B** a gamekeeper. ☐ **C** a farmer.

Speaking – Roleplay

2 **You and a classmate will play the roles of Sergeant Wilson and Cecil Barker. The person who plays the role of Sergeant Wilson should ask Cecil Barker questions about the crime, using the following words: What? When? Where? Who? What time?**

Vocabulary – Word Search

3 Look at the pictures of things seen at the crime scene. Find the words in the grid.

O	H	N	G	R	I	O	S
C	A	N	D	L	E	T	H
O	M	N	E	A	A	P	O
U	M	E	R	M	N	A	T
M	E	S	R	P	T	C	G
O	R	N	A	P	B	E	U
S	O	G	D	A	F	O	N
C	A	R	D	G	N	I	O
H	L	R	I	N	G	I	N
E	R	A	G	T	Z	S	E
A	M	T	A	D	L	I	A

V.V. 341

Writing ◆ 21st Century Skills

4 Write an article (140-190 words) about how police procedures and detectives' skills have changed since the times of Sherlock Holmes. What can detectives do nowadays to investigate crimes that they couldn't do in the 19th century? What role does science play in crime investigation now?

Pre-Reading Activities • PART 1: Chapter 3

Listening

▶ 5 **5** Listen to the start of **Chapter 3** and find the adjectives that describe the following nouns.

1 .... drawbridge

2 ...., ... moat

3 .... place

4 ...., ... window

5 .... border

6 .... weapon

PART 1:
THE TRAGEDY OF BIRLSTONE

Chapter 3

Holmes on the Scene

▶ 5 We walked through Birlstone village to the Manor House. As we looked at the long, low Jacobean house of red bricks, with yew trees on each side and a wooden drawbridge over the beautiful broad moat, I thought it was a very suitable place for a tragedy to happen.

'That's the window on the right,' said White Mason, 'It's open just as it was found last night.'

'It looks quite narrow for a man to get through,' commented Holmes.

'Yes, for a fat man. But you or I could get through it, Mr Holmes.'

Holmes examined the stone border of the moat, but there was no sign that anyone had climbed in or out of the dark water. The water was about three feet deep, not deep enough for a man to drown in. We all walked across the drawbridge and Ames, who was still shaking from the shock, opened the door. Mason told the village sergeant to go home and asked the butler to wait outside.

'We have to decide, gentlemen' said Mason, 'if the murder was done by someone outside or inside the house. If someone inside the house did the crime, it means they got this man down here and then killed him with a very noisy weapon – that nobody has seen in the house before. Not very probable, is it?' ▣

Birlstone Manor House was inspired by a real house with a moat in Groombridge in Kent, England.

Jacobean refers to the period when James the Sixth of Scotland and First of England was King.

Holmes and Watson arrive at Birlstone Manor.

30

▶ 6　Mason continued: 'Everyone agrees that, only a minute after the shot, everyone in the house came to this room, though Mr Cecil Barker said he was the first to arrive. In that short time, could the guilty person have made the footmarks in the corner, opened the window, marked the window sill with blood, and taken the wedding ring off the dead man's finger? It's impossible!'

I was impressed by this country policeman, who had a cool, clear brain and a solid idea of the facts. Holmes listened to him intently* and without his usual impatience.

'You put it very clearly,' said Holmes. 'I have to agree with you.'

White Mason went on: 'Well, that makes us think that it was done by someone from outside. In that case, it's still difficult, but not impossible. The man entered between four-thirty and six o'clock. Perhaps he was just a burglar, but it seems more likely that he had something against Mr Douglas. Mr Douglas spent most of his life in America and the shotgun is an American weapon. My theory is this: Mr Douglas entered the room and put down his candle. Mrs Douglas said that she heard the shot only a few minutes after her husband had left the bedroom. The candle was new and had only burnt down a little which also shows he was in the study only for a short time. A man appeared from behind the curtain, armed* with this gun, and demanded the wedding ring from Mr Douglas. In cold blood*, or during a struggle*, he shot Mr Douglas and dropped the gun and the strange card. Then, he escaped through the window and across the moat, just before Cecil Barker discovered the crime. How's that, Mr Holmes?'

'Very interesting,' said Holmes. 'but just a little unconvincing*.'

---

intently carefully
armed carrying a gun
in cold blood without any feeling of pity

struggle a fight
unconvincing not believable

'But Mr Holmes,' cried MacDonald. 'What else could have happened?'

'I would like a few more facts before I give you a theory, Mr Mac,' said Holmes, examining the body more closely. 'Can we have the butler in for a moment?'

Holmes asked Ames about the unusual mark branded* on Douglas's arm, but he didn't know what it meant. Did you notice anything strange about his behaviour yesterday, Ames?'

'He seemed to be a little restless* and excited, sir.'

'Ha! The attack may not have been entirely unexpected. We are making progress. What about this card with V.V. 341 written on it? Have you any cards like this in the house?'

'I don't think so, sir.'

Holmes walked across to the desk and tried out some of the ink and pens there.

'It wasn't printed in this room. Do you know anything about what's written here, Ames?' he said.

Ames replied that he had no idea. Inspector MacDonald and White Mason both thought it might be an indication of some secret society, just like the mark on the dead man's arm.

'The theory for the moment must be this,' explained Holmes. 'An agent from a secret society entered the house, waited for Mr Douglas and shot him in the head with this weapon. He escaped across the moat, after leaving a card, which would then be mentioned in the newspapers, telling other members of the society what he'd done. But why this gun, and why the missing ring?'

The others agreed with him.

---

branded marked with a hot iron   **restless** anxious, unable to relax

Sir Arthur Conan Doyle

Holmes went over to the window sill and examined the blood mark with his magnifying glass*. 'This has been made by a really broad* shoe, which is strange because it's very different from the footmark in the corner. What's this under the table?'

'Mr Douglas's dumb-bells,' said Ames.

'Dumb-bell – there's only one. Where's the other?'

Just then, Cecil Barker came in to say that the murderer's bicycle had been found in some bushes near the front door.

'Why did he leave it behind?' asked the inspector. 'We don't seem to have any answers yet in this case, Mr Holmes.'

'Don't we?' my friend answered thoughtfully. 'I wonder!'

Holmes and Inspector MacDonald decided to hear the evidence of the people in the house in the dining-room, starting with Ames. He told them that he had been employed by Mr Douglas as butler, when he first came to Birlstone five years before. He was a kind and considerate man, although not the type of employer Ames was used to. Ames said Mr Douglas seemed afraid of nothing. He ordered the drawbridge to be pulled up every night because he wanted to keep the ancient customs* of the old house. He didn't leave the village often, but on the day before the crime, he'd gone shopping in Tunbridge Wells. Ames had noticed that he was impatient and irritable that day, which was unusual for him. On the night of the crime, Ames was in the kitchen, when he heard the bell ring violently. He heard no shot but said it was unlikely he would have, because the kitchen was at the very back of the house. The housekeeper had also heard the bell ringing and had come out of her room. They'd gone to the front of the house together. As they reached the bottom of the stairs, he'd seen

Dumb-bell is an old word for a hand weight and is usually used in pairs. The origin of the word comes from 16th century England when athletes trained with handheld bells with the clappers removed to stop them making a noise, and so made the bells 'dumb'.

Tunbridge Wells is a town in the county of Kent, east of the county of Sussex, where the fictional Birlstone is situated.

magnifying glass

broad wide
customs traditions

Mrs Douglas coming down. She hadn't seemed agitated*. When she reached the bottom of the stairs, Mr Barker had rushed out of the study to stop her and begged* her to go back upstairs.

'Poor Jack is dead!' he cried. 'You can do nothing. Please go back!'

Mrs Allen, the housekeeper, had taken her upstairs to her bedroom and stayed with her.

Ames and Mr Barker had returned to the study. The candle was no longer lit, but the lamp was burning. They had looked out of the window, but it was dark and they had heard and seen nothing. Ames had then lowered the drawbridge and Mr Barker had gone to get the police.

'Jack' is a name often used by friends or family members for someone called 'John'.

Mrs Allen agreed with what Ames had said. She hadn't heard the shot either, but said she had heard a sound, about half an hour before, which seemed like a door slamming*. The other servants had heard nothing and only found out what had happened when the police arrived.

Cecil Barker was questioned next. He was convinced the murderer had escaped through the window, as shown by the bloodstain* on the window sill and the fact that the drawbridge had been up. He had his own theory about the murder. Douglas never spoke about some parts of his life. He'd gone to America when he was very young and had made a lot of money. Barker had met him in California where they'd become partners in a successful gold mine in a place called Benito Canyon. But Douglas had suddenly sold his share* and returned to England. He was a widower at the time. Later, Barker had also sold his part in the business and met up with Douglas again in London.

---

agitated nervous, upset
beg (here) to ask someone to do something (with emotion)

slam to close a door violently
bloodstain mark left by blood
share a part (in a business)

Douglas had given him the impression that he was in danger from some secret society that wanted to kill him, which explained perhaps the writing on the card.

'Do you know where his first wife came from?' asked Holmes.

'No, but I remember she was German and had died of typhoid the year before I met him.'

'Had he been in any other parts of America?'

'I heard him talk about Chicago. He had worked there and knew it well. He also talked about the coal and iron districts*. He had travelled a lot.'

'Did this secret society have something to do with politics or criminals?'

'Absolutely not. He was the most honest man I'd ever met. He liked to stay away from other people. That's why I first thought that someone was looking for him. Then when he left suddenly for Europe, I was sure. Just a week later, some dangerous-looking men came to the mine to ask about him.'

'Were these men from California?'

'I'm not sure. But they were Americans, and they weren't miners. That was almost seven years ago.'

'Why did he not ask the police for protection?'

'Perhaps there was nobody who could protect him from this danger,' said Barker. 'In fact, he always carried a revolver* in his pocket. It's just bad luck that last night he was in his dressing gown and had left it in his bedroom. I suppose he thought he was safe in his house once the drawbridge was up.'

Typhoid is a fatal illness caused by bacteria in contaminated food and water. In the late 19th century, thousands of people died in America and Europe due to poor sanitation.

district area of a country or city

revolver

'So, to be clear,' said MacDonald. 'Douglas left California six years ago, and you followed him a year later?'

'Yes, I returned a month before his marriage. I was his best man,'

'Did you know Mrs Douglas before her marriage?'

'No, I didn't. I had been away from England for ten years.'

'But you have seen a lot of her since. Did Mr Douglas approve of your friendship with his wife?'

'I have seen a lot of them both,' Barker answered angrily. 'What has this to do with your investigation? Poor Douglas could be jealous, but he was fond of me and devoted* to his wife. You must understand that his wife was faithful* to him, and I was a loyal friend.'

Barker spoke very passionately but Inspector MacDonald continued with the subject.

'You know that the dead man's wedding ring had been taken? This could suggest, whoever may have removed it, that the marriage and the tragedy were connected.'

'I don't know what it means,' replied Barker. 'But I think you have the wrong idea.'

Inspector MacDonald then asked him why he had blown out the candle on the table and lit the lamp on the table. Barker explained that the candle hadn't been bright enough.

The next witness was Mrs Douglas. I didn't expect her to be so calm after the tragic events. She was pale and her eyes were sad, but this young, beautiful woman was very composed*. She confirmed everything that Cecil Barker and Ames had told us.

'Can you tell us how long your husband had been downstairs before you heard the shot?' 'No, I couldn't say. He was nervous of fire, so he checked the house every night.'

The best man at a wedding is usually a relation or good friend of the groom (the man who is getting married) who is a legal witness at the ceremony.

House fires were a common risk in the 19th century. Many houses were built using a lot of wood, and the use of candle and oil lamps for light and wood or coal fires for heat increased the possibility of accidents happening.

devoted very loving
faithful (here) never having relationships with other men

composed calm

'Had he ever spoken about anything that had happened in America to make him feel he was in danger?'

Mrs Douglas thought carefully before she answered. 'Yes. I've always felt that he was in danger, but he refused to discuss it with me. He probably didn't want me to worry, but I knew from the way he behaved and certain words that he said.'

'May I ask,' asked Holmes. 'what words made you think he was in danger?'

'The Valley of Fear,' the lady answered. 'That was an expression he used when I questioned him. His words were 'I have been in the Valley of Fear. I am not out of it yet. Sometimes I think that we never will be.' I asked him what he meant, but he didn't explain. I think it was some real valley where something terrible had happened to him.'

'And he never mentioned any names?'

'Yes, once when he had a fever*, he spoke angrily about someone called Bodymaster McGinty. I'm sure there is a connection between this man and the Valley of Fear.'

Mrs Douglas was probably not aware that Dr Watson had seen her smile. This could indicate that she knows something about why the wedding ring was not on the dead man's finger.

'Why do you think his wedding ring was taken?' Holmes asked, and for a moment I thought I saw a faint smile on the woman's lips. 'I really don't know,' she answered.

When Mrs Douglas left the room, Holmes rang the bell to call Ames again.

'Ames, can you remember what Mr Barker was wearing on his feet last night?'

'Yes, Mr Holmes. He was wearing slippers. They're still under the chair in the hall.'

---

fever a high body temperature

Holmes brought the slippers into the study, and we saw that the soles* were dark with blood.

'Strange!' murmured* Holmes. He placed the slipper on the blood mark on the window sill. It was exactly the same. He smiled in silence at his colleagues.

'There's no doubt then!' cried the inspector. 'Barker marked the window sill himself. But why, Mr Holmes?' ■

sole (here) the part under a shoe that touches the ground

murmur to say something quietly

Reading   B2 FIRST

1 **Read Chapter 3 again and choose the correct answer A, B, C or D.**

1 After the shot, who was the first person to arrive at the study?
- ☐ **A** Ames
- ☐ **B** Cecil Barker
- ☐ **C** Mrs Douglas
- ☐ **D** Sergeant Wilson

2 According to Sherlock Holmes, who could have shot John Douglas?
- ☐ **A** a burglar
- ☐ **B** Cecil Barker
- ☐ **C** Douglas himself
- ☐ **D** a secret society member

3 What did Sherlock find under the table?
- ☐ **A** a dumb-bell
- ☐ **B** a bloodstain
- ☐ **C** a boot print
- ☐ **D** a gun

4 What did Ames hear when he was in the kitchen?
- ☐ **A** a gunshot
- ☐ **B** a bell ringing
- ☐ **C** a door slamming
- ☐ **D** Barker coming downstairs

5 Where had Cecil Barker first met John Douglas?
- ☐ **A** London
- ☐ **B** Chicago
- ☐ **C** California
- ☐ **D** Germany

6 Why did John Douglas check the house every night?
- ☐ **A** He was nervous about fires.
- ☐ **B** He was afraid of burglars.
- ☐ **C** He checked all the windows were closed.
- ☐ **D** He put out all the lamps.

Grammar – Phrasal Verbs

2 **Choose a phrasal verb from the box that has the same meaning as the verb in brackets, and insert it in the correct sentence in a suitable tense.**

> find out - take off - blow out - try out

1 The murderer .... (remove) the dead man's wedding ring.

2 Holmes .... (test) some of the pens in the study.

3 The servants .... (discover) what had happened when the police arrived.

4 Cecil Barker .... (extinguish) the candle when he went into the study.

Speaking

3 After reading the witness statements in **Chapter 3**, think about all the evidence at the crime scene, discuss with a partner and give your own theory about the murder of **John Douglas**. Name the evidence 1-5. What do you think it means?

1 ....

V.V. 341

2 ....

3 ....

4 ....

5 ....

Pre-Reading Activities • PART 1: Chapter 4

Listening

▶ 7 **4 A** Listen to the start of **Chapter 4**. After hearing **Dr Watson's** conversation with **Cecil Barker** and **Mrs Douglas**, have you changed your mind about the theory you gave in **Speaking no.3**?

4 B At the end of the next chapter, **Sherlock Holmes** gives the solution to the mystery. Before you read it, discuss the clues in the previous 3 chapters with a partner, and give your own solutions.

PART 1:
THE TRAGEDY OF BIRLSTONE

Chapter 4

The Truth Comes Out

▶ 7 I decided to return to the inn and leave the detectives to discuss the case. But first, I went for a walk in the gardens. As I walked towards the hedge of yew trees, I heard voices from the other side: the deep voice of a man and the light laughter of a woman. When I looked around the hedge, I saw Mr Barker and Mrs Douglas sitting on a bench. I was shocked to see that the look of sadness on the lady's face had gone and that she and Barker were now smiling happily. When they saw me there, they became serious again. The shock on my face was obvious to them.

'You must think I'm very hard-hearted,' said Mrs Douglas. 'Perhaps one day you will understand. If you only realised____' she started to say.

Then she said, 'Please, Dr Watson. I'd like to ask you a question. You know Mr Holmes better than anyone. If he was told something in confidence*, would it be necessary for him to pass this information on to the police?'

'Mr Holmes is a private investigator,' I replied. 'He makes his own judgements, but he wouldn't hide anything from the detectives that could help them catch a criminal. You'd have to ask Mr Holmes himself.' I then raised my hat and left them sitting on the bench. ■

in confidence as a secret
not to be told to others

Watson surprises Barker
and Mrs Douglas.

42

▶ 8 Later when I told Holmes what had happened, he confirmed what I had told them. He said it could create difficulties if there were arrests.

'Do you think that's likely?' I asked him.

'My dear Watson, I'll tell you once I know more, and when we have found the missing dumb-bell.'

'The dumb-bell!' I exclaimed*.

'Dear me, Watson, have you not understood that the missing dumb-bell is important in this case? An athlete would never use just one dumb-bell! The story told by Mr Barker is a lie, but it's also confirmed by Mrs Douglas. So, she's lying too. But why? Let's try, Watson, to find out the truth.

'According to what we've been told, after the murder, the killer had less than a minute to take the wedding ring from the dead man's finger, and put the card beside his victim. Obviously impossible! He could have taken the ring before he killed the man, but as the candle had been lit only a short time, this is impossible. The killer must have been alone with the dead man for some time with the lamp lit. I'm very sure of that. As the gunshot was definitely the cause of death, it must have been fired earlier than we were told. As there could have been no mistake about this, it proves that there is a conspiracy* between Mr Barker and Mrs Douglas. I also proved that the blood mark on the window sill was made by Barker. So, things look bad for him. Now, we have to ask ourselves what time the murder actually happened. Up to half past ten, the servants were moving about the house so it was certainly not before then. The sound the housekeeper

Dr Watson is always surprised at the simple things or facts that seem unimportant but are important to Sherlock.

If the candle had been lit for a long time, while the killer was taking the wedding ring off, it would have burnt down more and been shorter. This makes Cecil Barker's evidence even more unbelievable.

---

exclaim to shout out in surprise or with emotion

conspiracy a secret plan to do something against the law

The Valley of Fear

heard, half an hour before the alarm was given, was most probably the gunshot, and this was the real time of the murder. If Mrs Douglas and Mr Barker aren't the real murderers, what were they doing from quarter to eleven, when they heard the real shot, until quarter past eleven, when they rang the bell to call the servants?'

'Sadly, I too think that there is some conspiracy between them and that they know more than they have said,' said Dr Watson. 'Mrs Douglas must be heartless to be laughing with Mr Barker just a few hours after her husband's murder.'

'Exactly!' agreed Holmes. 'And the fact that she allowed the housekeeper to take her away when her husband's body was found shows that this was pre-arranged. In my experience, no wife who really loved her husband would allow anyone to stop her from seeing him.'

'You think, then, that Barker and Mrs Douglas are definitely guilty of the murder?' asked Dr Watson.

'You're very direct, Watson. I believe they know the truth, and are conspiring* to hide it, but I'm not sure they're the killers. If we assume that everything they've said is false, that means there was never any danger from a secret society or Valley of Fear. But why was an American shotgun used? And why was the wedding ring removed?'

'There may have been a terrible secret in Douglas's life, perhaps at the time of his first marriage, which explains why the ring was taken. The killer could have still been in the study when Barker and Mrs Douglas arrived and perhaps he convinced them to let him go to avoid the secret being revealed*.'

'And how do you think you can prove this?'

conspire to make secret plans together   reveal to uncover, show

45

'I think an evening in the room alone would help me a lot. Do you have your big umbrella with you, Watson?' said Holmes, mysteriously.

Later that evening, Inspector MacDonald and White Mason returned with some news. Since Mr Douglas had seemed more worried on his return from Tunbridge Wells, they had taken the bicycle to all the hotels there to find the owner. One of the hotel managers had said it belonged to a man named Hargrave, who had stayed in the hotel two days before. He had come from London but had given no address. He only had a bicycle and a small suitcase. The man was an American of about fifty, tall with grey hair and a grey moustache. He had a curved* nose and a fierce-looking face, and he was wearing a grey suit and a yellow coat.

'That might almost be the description of Douglas himself,' said Holmes. 'I'm going to do some investigating myself now.'

'Can we help you Mr Holmes?'

'No, no! Darkness and Dr Watson's umbrella are all I need'

The next morning, we met Inspector MacDonald and White Mason at the local police station.

'I advise you to abandon the case,' said Holmes.

They looked at him in amazement. 'But this cyclist must be somewhere. Why shouldn't we get him? You agreed with us last night. You're holding something back, Mr Holmes!'

The inspector was annoyed.

'You know the way I work, Mr Mac. I never tell you my theory until I'm sure it's correct. I can only tell you that I was at the Manor House last night. Ames took me to the study and didn't tell anyone else.

curved not straight, bent

I was looking for the missing dumb-bell and I found it.'

'Where?'

'I can't tell you that yet. Let me investigate a little more, and then I promise I'll tell you everything.'

'Can we do anything?' asked the inspector.

'You can write a note to Mr Barker. Here's what it should say.'

> *Dear Sir,*
>
> *I think we should drain* the moat, in the hope that we may find something which could be useful for our investigation. I have asked the workmen to be there early tomorrow morning. I thought it best to explain this to you beforehand*.'*

'Now sign that and send it by hand about four o'clock. At that hour we shall meet again here.'

When we all met later, Holmes was very serious, I was curious, and the detectives obviously annoyed. We walked to the Manor House and hid behind the hedges on the opposite side of the moat so that we could watch the study window. Then we waited.

'Why are we here? You should really tell us what we are doing?' asked MacDonald, angrily.

Holmes laughed. 'I only ask a little patience, Mr Mac, and all will be clear to you.'

Finally, after waiting a long time in the cold, still darkness, we saw a shadow pass in front of the lamp in the study. The window opened and we saw a man looking out into the garden. Then, he leaned

---

drain to empty something by taking liquid out

beforehand before an action or event

The fact that the house is surrounded by a moat plays an important part in the mystery.

forward, put his hand into the moat and pulled out a large round object.

'Now!' cried Holmes. 'Now!'

We all ran across the bridge to the house. Holmes rang the bell furiously. When Ames opened the door, we all rushed into the study and saw Barker with the lamp in his hand.

'What's the meaning of all this?' he cried. 'What are you here for?'

Holmes looked around the room and saw a wet bundle* tied with a cord*, under the table.

'This is what we are here for, Mr Barker – this bundle weighted with a dumb-bell, which you've just taken out of the moat.'

Barker stared at Holmes in amazement. 'How did you know?' he asked.

'I wondered why a dumb-bell was missing and supposed that, with the moat nearby, it could have been used to sink something into the water. I found this bundle last night. I pulled it out with Watson's umbrella and inspected it, before putting it back. Then I had to prove who had placed it there, by announcing that the moat would be drained tomorrow.'

Holmes put the wet bundle on the table and opened it up. He took out the dumb-bell and a pair of boots. Then, he laid on the table a long knife, some underwear, socks, a grey suit, and a yellow coat.

'The clothes seem ordinary, except for the yellow coat,' said Holmes. 'As you can see, it has a label* – 'Neal, Outfitter, Vermissa, USA.' Vermissa is a little town in the United States, an area that Douglas's first wife came from. So, the V. V. on the card could stand

---

bundle a collection of things wrapped in a cloth

cord

label a tag with writing on it

for Vermissa Valley, and perhaps be the Valley of Fear we have heard of. And now, Mr Barker, perhaps you could tell us more.'

'You know such a lot, Mr Holmes, perhaps you had better tell us some more,' said Barker.

'No doubt, Mr Barker, but it would be better to hear it from you.'

'Well, all I can say is that if there's any secret here, it's not my secret to tell.'

Just then, Mrs Douglas, who'd been listening at the half-opened door, came into the room.

'You've done enough for now, Cecil,' she said.

'More than enough,' said Holmes. 'I have every sympathy* for you, madam, but I'd ask you to trust the police. There's so much to explain, and I think it's best that you let Mr Douglas tell us his own story.'

Hearing these words, Mrs Douglas cried out in amazement, as we all did when, from a dark corner of the room, we saw a man appear.

'It's best this way, Jack,' his wife said. 'I'm sure that it's best.'

'Indeed, yes, Mr Douglas,' said Sherlock Holmes. 'I'm sure that you'll find it best.'

The man stood looking at us and then, he came towards me and handed me some papers. 'I've heard of you, Dr Watson. I bet* you've never heard a story like this before. Tell it your own way, but these are the facts. I've spent the last two days writing it down. You may have it - you and your readers. Here's the story of the Valley of Fear.'

'That's the past, Mr Douglas,' said Sherlock Holmes quietly. 'We'd now like to hear your story of the present.'

Vermissa Valley is a fictional place in the USA, and is very important in the second part of the story.

sympathy feeling of pity for someone's bad luck

bet (here) to be sure

Inspector MacDonald, who'd been staring at the man in amazement, cried out at last.

'If you are Mr Douglas of Birlstone Manor, then who is the dead man? And where have you been?'

'Ah, Mr Mac,' said Holmes. 'This old house has excellent hiding places. When I found the clothes last night, I knew the body couldn't have been Mr Douglas, but the cyclist from Tunbridge Wells. I realised that Mr Douglas was probably hidden in the house.'

'You're right,' said Douglas. 'but I've done nothing to be ashamed of. However, you can judge that for yourselves. My story is written there.' He pointed to the papers. 'Some men have good reason to hate me, and as long as they're alive, I'm not safe. They chased me from Chicago to California, and out of America, but when I married and came here, I thought I could live in peace. However, two days ago, I was in Tunbridge Wells when I recognised a man called Baldwin who'd been chasing me for years. So, I came home and prepared for trouble. At home, when the drawbridge was up, I felt safe, but that night when I went into the study, I saw a boot under the curtain. The man attacked me with the knife, so I hit him with the hammer, knocking the knife to the floor. When he took the shotgun from under his coat, I tried to take it from him and he was shot in the face. Barker and my wife came running down. It was then that I had a brilliant idea. The man had the same mark on his arm as I have, and looked similar to me. So, Barker and I changed his clothes with mine and put his into the moat in a bundle with the dumb-bell. The card he was going to lay on my body was lying beside him. I put my rings on his fingers,

Old English houses often had hiding places. During the time of Queen Elizabeth I, when Roman Catholic priests were often imprisoned, tortured and even killed, the hiding places were called 'priest holes'. During the English Civil War (1642-51), they were used by Royalists who supported King Charles I to avoid being killed by the Roundheads led by Oliver Cromwell.

except the wedding ring which I couldn't get off my finger. I thought I could hide until things calmed down. The others would read in the newspapers that Baldwin had killed me, and that would be an end to my problems. So, that's the whole truth. I ask you now, what happens under English law?'

'You will be treated fairly under English law, Mr Douglas. But it's not over* yet, I fear,' said Holmes seriously. 'I advise you to be careful.' ⬛

Mr Douglas did not mean to kill the man. He was only defending himself. But he is worried that he will be sent to prison or even executed. The death penalty in Britain still existed until 1965.

over (here) finished

Grammar B2 FIRST

1 **Complete the text with one word for each space.**

Holmes was convinced **(1)** .... Cecil Barker and Mrs
Douglas knew more **(2)** .... the murder of John Douglas
(3) .... they had said. He had proved that the footprint in
the blood **(4)** .... the window sill had been made by Barker's
slipper. He also believed it would have **(5)** .... impossible
for the killer to remove the dead man's ring in the short time
(6) .... the shot being heard and Barker finding Douglas's
body. This meant that the gun could have been fired long
(7) .... the body was found and so, Barker and Mrs Douglas
were lying about hearing the shot and running downstairs. In fact, the sound
the housekeeper **(8)** .... half an hour before must have
been the shot. So, what were they **(9)** .... in that time
before they **(10)** .... the bell to call the servants?

Vocabulary

2 **Make nouns from the following adjectives.**

1	deep	....
2	sad	....
3	difficult	....
4	important	....
5	true	....
6	curious	....
7	patient	....
8	amazed	....
9	dark	....
10	possible	....
11	safe	....
12	guilty	....

Reading

3 Decide if the following sentences are True (T) or False (F).

	T	F
1 The Inspector's letter said that the moat would be drained at 4 o'clock.	☐	☐
2 When Holmes rushed into the study, Barker was holding a lamp.	☐	☐
3 The dumb-bell had been used as a weight.	☐	☐
4 In the bundle there was a grey coat.	☐	☐
5 Mr Douglas gave Dr Watson the story he'd written about his past.	☐	☐
6 Cecil Barker had killed the man in the study.	☐	☐

Vocabulary

4 In the bundle found in the moat, there were some things belonging to the dead man. Look at the pictures below and identify them.

1 ....

2 ....

3 ....

4 ....

5 ....

6 ....

Pre-Reading Activities • PART 2: Chapter 1

Speaking

5 In Chapter 4 of Part 1, the clues to the murder of a man called Baldwin included a card with strange letters and numbers on it, an American shotgun and a secret symbol on the arm of the dead man. The title of Part 2 is 'The Scowrers'. What do you think they are? What connection is there between the dead man and John Douglas? What secret does John Douglas's past hold? Discuss with a partner.

PART 2:
THE SCOWRERS

Chapter 1

The Man

▶ 9 And now, my readers, I want to take you back twenty years in time and thousands of miles away, to tell you a terrible story that you may find hard to believe. This will bring an end to the story of the man known as John Douglas.

John Douglas was really an Irish immigrant who had been living in America, and this part tells us the story of his past and explains the mystery in the first part of the novel.

In February 1875, a young Irishman, of about 30, was on a train, travelling through the deep snow to Vermissa Valley, the most desolate* part of the United States, where men came to work in the coal and iron mines to make their fortune. He had a handsome face and looked like a sociable, friendly person, but there was also a tough side to him.

In the carriage*, there were miners returning from a day's work. They sat talking in low voices, sometimes looking over at two policemen on the opposite side. Occasionally the young man pulled some papers out of his pocket, and also a large revolver from the back of his waist, to look at them. This was noticed by a worker sitting opposite him.

'Hello, mate*!' he said. 'I see you're ready for anything.'

The young man looked embarrassed and smiled.

---

desolate miserable and empty
carriage part of a train where passengers travel

mate friend, pal

'Yes,' he said. 'We need them sometimes in Chicago, the place I have just come from.'

'You may find you need it here too. Why have you come here?'

'I heard there was work for a willing man.'

'Are you a member of the union*?' asked the workman.

'I'm one of the Eminent Order of Freemen. Every town has a lodge* and I'm sure I'll find friends here too.'

These words had an effect on the workman. He looked around suspiciously at the others in the carriage. The miners were still whispering among themselves and the two policemen were sleeping. Then he came across and sat beside the young Irishman.

The man held out his hand to see if the young man would use the secret handshake.

'I see you speak the truth,' he said. 'But it's better to make certain.'

He then raised his right hand to his right eyebrow, and the young man did the same.

'Dark nights are unpleasant,' said the workman.

'Yes, for strangers to travel,' the other answered.

'That's good enough. I'm Brother Scanlan, Lodge 341, Vermissa Valley. Glad to see you here.'

'Thank you. I'm Brother John McMurdo, Lodge 29, Chicago. I'm lucky to meet a brother so early.'

'Well, there are plenty of us right here in Vermissa Valley. Why can't a Freeman find work in Chicago?'

'I found plenty of work,' said McMurdo.

'Then why did you leave?'

Members of secret societies used secret gestures* and words to check that they were speaking to a fellow* Brother.

---

union (here) society of workmen
lodge meeting place for secret societies

gesture a movement made with your hand
fellow sharing a particular activity of quality with someone

McMurdo nodded towards the policemen. 'I guess those chaps* would be glad to know,' he said.

Scanlan groaned* sympathetically. 'In trouble?' he asked in a whisper.

'I have my own good reasons for leaving Chicago,' he said angrily.

'All right, mate, no offence meant. It doesn't matter what you've done. Where are you going now?'

McMurdo took out an envelope and held it close to a dirty oil lamp. 'Here's the address—Jacob Shafter, Sheridan Street. It's a boarding house* recommended by a man I knew in Chicago.'

'Well, I don't know it, but I live at Hobson's Patch. This is my station here, but I'll give you some advice: if you're in trouble in Vermissa, go straight to the Union House and see Boss McGinty, the Bodymaster of Vermissa Lodge. Goodbye, mate! Remember: if you're in trouble, go to Boss McGinty.'

Scanlan got off the train, and while McMurdo sat thinking, he heard a voice. It was one of the policemen.

'I guess you are new to this area, young man?'

'Well, what if I am?' McMurdo answered roughly.

'Just this, mister, that I should advise you not to make friends with Mike Scanlan or his gang*.'

'I'm new to the place; but I'm not new to you and your kind!' cried McMurdo angrily. 'You're the same in all places, and giving advice when nobody asks for it.'

There was a look of admiration from the other miners on the train because of the way he spoke to the policemen, and when McMurdo got off at his station, one of them offered to show him the way to

chap (informal) a person, a guy
groan to make a deep sound showing pain

boarding house a place with rooms for rent
gang an organised group of criminals

Sir Arthur Conan Doyle

This is the description of a typical town in the mining valleys of America. The centres were full of saloons, or bars, that made money from the men who came from all over the country to work in the mines there.

Shafter's boarding house. The town of Vermissa was depressing and ugly. The numerous* gas-lamps lit up streets of muddy snow, lined with* dirty wooden houses, each with its veranda facing the street. As they approached the centre of the town, the scene was brightened by a row of well-lit stores, and even more by a group of saloons*, in which the miners spent their hard-earned but generous wages*.

'That's the Union House,' said the guide, pointing to one saloon which looked like a hotel. 'Jack McGinty is the boss there.'

'What sort of a man is he?' McMurdo asked.

'What! have you never heard of the boss?'

'How could I have heard of him when you know that I am a stranger in these parts?'

'Well, I thought his name was known all over the country. It's been in the newspapers often enough.'

Scowrers is the fictional name for a criminal gang, based on a real group of young Irishmen, called the Molly Maguires who rebelled against the destruction of Ireland's farming industry and corrupt landlords by destroying farms and attacking land agents.

The miner lowered his voice—'over the affairs of the Scowrers.'

'I remember reading about the Scowrers in Chicago. A gang of murderers, are they not?'

'Quiet!' cried the miner, staring in amazement at his companion. 'Man, you won't live long in these parts if you speak in the open street like that. Many men have been killed for less.'

'Well, I know nothing about them. Only what I have read.'

'And I'm not saying that you've not read the truth.'

The man looked nervously round him as he spoke. 'But don't you dare to breathe* the name of Jack McGinty in connection with murder, stranger, for every whisper goes back to him. There's the house you're looking for. You'll find old Jacob Shafter is one of the most honest men in this town.'

numerous many
lined with with buildings on either side of the street
saloon a bar, typical of the old West in America

wages money earned from working
breathe (here) to say, speak about

'Thank you,' said McMurdo, shaking hands with the man, and he walked up to the house and knocked on the door. It was opened at once by a young and very beautiful woman. She looked German, with blonde hair and beautiful dark eyes. She looked at the stranger with surprise and blushed*. Framed* in the bright light of the open doorway, it seemed to McMurdo that he had never seen a more beautiful picture. He stood staring without a word, and finally she said, in a slight German accent.

'I thought it was father. Did you come to see him? I expect him back soon.'

'No, miss,' he said at last, 'But your house was recommended to me for board. I thought it might suit me—and now I know it will.'

'Come right in, sir,' she said. 'I'm Miss Ettie Shafter, Mr Shafter's daughter. I run the house. Ah, here is my father! You can arrange things with him.'

McMurdo explained his business and, for seven dollars a week paid in advance, he got a room with the Shafters; the first step which led to a long and dark train of events, ending in a far distant land.

The events that follow the young Irishman's arrival in Vermissa lead to what happens many miles away in England thirty years later.

Within* a week McMurdo had become the most important person at Shafter's. When he and the other boarders* gathered together in the evening, this young Irishman's conversation was the brightest and his singing the best. But he showed again and again his ability to get angry suddenly and also a contempt* for the police, which delighted some and frightened others. Every day he told Ettie Shafter he loved her. Even when she told him there was someone else, he insisted

blush to become red in the face
framed surrounded by something like in a picture
within (here) before the end of

boarder (here) person who pays rent for a room
contempt dislike, hate

that one day she would say yes to him. McMurdo got a job as a book-keeper*; for he was a well- educated man. This kept him out most of the day, and he hadn't had a chance yet to visit the head of the lodge of the Eminent Order of Freemen. He was reminded of this omission*, however, by a visit one evening from Mike Scanlan, the fellow member he had met on the train.

'Hello, McMurdo,' he said, 'I remembered your address, so I thought I'd visit you. I'm surprised you've not reported to the Bodymaster. Why haven't you seen Boss McGinty yet?'

'Well, I had to find a job. I've been busy.'

'You must find time for him! You should have gone to the Union House the first morning after you came here!'

McMurdo was surprised. 'I've been a member of the lodge for over two years, Scanlan, but I've never heard that it was so urgent to do that.'

'Maybe not in Chicago.'

'Well, it's the same society here. Isn't it?'

Scanlan stared at him. There was something sinister* in his eyes.

'Tell me that in a month's time,' he said. 'I hear you had a talk with a policeman after I left the train.'

'How did you know that?'

'Oh, it got about—things do get about here.'

'Well, yes. I told them what I thought of them.'

'McGinty will like you!'

'Why, does he hate the police too?'

Scanlan burst out laughing*. 'You go and see him, my lad*,' he said,

book-keeper accountant
omission action of leaving out something
sinister dark, evil

burst out laughing to start laughing suddenly
lad boy, young man

as he left. 'It's not the police but you that he'll hate if you don't! Now, take a friend's advice and go at once!'

That evening Mr Shafter came to him and asked him about Ettie. McMurdo confirmed that he was in love with his daughter, but that he knew there was another man interested in her.

'Did she tell you who it was?' asked Mr Shafter.

'No, I asked her; but she wouldn't tell.'

'Perhaps she didn't want to frighten you away. It's Teddy Baldwin, a boss of Scowrers.'

'Scowrers! I've heard of them before, and always in a whisper! What are you all afraid of? Who are they?' shouted McMurdo, angrily.

Mr Shafter lowered his voice. 'The Scowrers,' he said, 'are the Eminent Order of Freemen!'

The young man stared. 'Why, I am a member of that order* myself.'

'You! I would never have had you in my house if I had known that.'

'What's wrong with the order? It's for charity* and good fellowship*. The rules say so,' protested McMurdo.

'Maybe in some places. But here it's a murder society,' whispered Mr Shafter.

McMurdo laughed in disbelief. 'How can you prove that?' he asked.

'Prove it? There are around fifty murders to prove it! Everyone in this valley knows it!'

'Look!' said McMurdo earnestly*. 'I belong to a society that I know only as an innocent one, all over the United States. I think you owe* me either an apology or else an explanation, Mr Shafter.'

'I can only tell you what the whole world knows, mister.'

order (here) group of people in a society
charity raising money for those in need
fellowship having a common interest
earnestly seriously
owe be obliged to do / give something

'That's just gossip—I want proof!' said McMurdo.

'If you live here long enough, you will get your proof. But you are one of them. You'll soon be as bad as the rest. You have to find other lodgings*, mister. Is it not bad enough that Baldwin is courting* my Ettie, and that I dare not turn* him down? You can't sleep here after tonight!'

Ted Baldwin is a member of the Vermissa Lodge and one of the Scowrers. All of the good people in Vermissa are afraid of them and can do nothing to stop them.

That same evening, McMurdo spoke to Ettie.

'Your father has told me to leave,' he said. 'But, Ettie, even though I've only known you for a week, I know that I can't live without you!'

'Please don't say that Jack!' she said, covering her face with her hands. 'You're too late. I've made a promise to another.'

McMurdo took her white hand in his own strong ones.

'Will you ruin your life and mine for the sake of* a promise? Follow your heart! Say you'll be mine and we'll face the situation together!'

'It could not be here, Jack. Could you take me away?'

'No, Ettie, I can't leave here. What is there to be afraid of?'

'You don't know Jack. You've been here too short a time. You don't know this Baldwin. You don't know McGinty and his Scowrers!'

'No, I don't know them. I don't fear them, and I don't believe in them!' said McMurdo. 'If these men, as your father says, have done numerous crimes in the valley, and if everyone knows them by name, why have none been brought to justice?'

'Because no witness dares to appear against them. He wouldn't live a month if he did. Also, their own men swear* that the accused one was far from the scene of the crime. But surely, Jack, you have read all this in the newspapers!' exclaimed Ettie.

lodgings room(s) to rent
court old word meaning to get to know someone you want to marry

turn down (here) say no to
for the sake of because of
swear to declare formally, promise

'Maybe these men have no other way to help themselves.'

'Oh, Jack, don't speak like that! That's how Baldwin speaks. And that's why I hate him so much! But I'm also afraid of him. And I fear for my father too. It would be dangerous for me to tell Baldwin how I really feel about him. But if you could run away with me, Jack, we could take father with us and live forever far from the power of these wicked* men.'

'No harm shall come to you or your father, Ettie. But you know so little about me. You may soon find out that I'm as bad as him.'

'No, no, Jack! I would trust you anywhere.'

The door opened suddenly, and a young fellow* came in: a handsome young man of about the same age and build* as McMurdo himself. Under his large black hat, a handsome face with fierce eyes and a curved nose looked angrily at Jack and Ettie.

It was Ted Baldwin. 'Who is this?' he asked abruptly*.

'He's a friend, a new boarder* here,' replied Ettie. 'Mr McMurdo, may I introduce you to Mr Baldwin?'

The young men nodded in an unfriendly way to each other.

'Maybe Miss Ettie has told you how it is with us?' said Baldwin.

'I didn't understand that there was any relation between you.'

'Didn't you?' said Baldwin, looking annoyed. 'Well, you can understand it now. You can take it from me that this young lady is mine, and you'll find it a very fine evening for a walk.'

'Thank you, I am in no mood for a walk,' replied McMurdo.

'Aren't you? Maybe you're in the mood for a fight, Mr Boarder!'

McMurdo tries to excuse the Scowrers for their actions. This is a reference to Union problems in Ireland and America, when groups of people used violence to defend the rights of the workers.

wicked evil
fellow a man or boy
build (here) size and shape of body

abruptly suddenly and rudely
boarder person who stays in a boarding house

'I think, Ettie, that if you were to leave us alone, we could get this thing settled,' said McMurdo quietly. 'Or maybe, Mr Baldwin, you will come out into the street with me?'

'I'll get even with* you without even getting my hands dirty,' said his enemy. 'See here!'

He rolled up his sleeve. On his arm was a strange sign: a circle with a triangle inside it. 'Do you know what that means?'

This is the same sign that the dead man at Birlstone Manor had on his arm, the man we know now was Ted Baldwin. He is showing it to McMurdo to prove he is a Scowrer and so it would be dangerous to go against him.

'I neither know nor care!' replied McMurdo calmly.

'Well, you will know, I'll promise you that. As to you, Ettie, you'll come back to me and then I'll tell you what your punishment may be!' He left, banging* the door behind him.

For a few moments McMurdo and the girl stood in silence. Then she threw her arms around him.

'Oh, Jack, how brave you were! But, you must leave tonight! What chance have you got against them, with Boss McGinty and all the power of the lodge behind them?'

'Don't be afraid for me. I'm a Freeman too.'

Ettie loves Jack, but she knows that it is dangerous to go against Ted Baldwin and the Scowrers

'But if you're a Freeman, Jack, why not go down and speak to Boss McGinty? Oh, hurry, Jack, hurry!'

'I was thinking the same thing,' said McMurdo. 'I'll go right now and fix* it.' ◼

---

get even with to take revenge on
bang to close a door violently,
making a loud noise

fix (here) to deal with a situation

Reading   **B2 FIRST**

1 **Read Chapter 1 again and choose the correct answer A, B, C or D.**

1 Vermissa Valley was known for its...
- ☐ **A** gold mines.
- ☐ **B** coal mines.
- ☐ **C** tin mines.
- ☐ **D** diamond mines.

2 How did the miners travel to work?
- ☐ **A** In a carriage.
- ☐ **B** By bus.
- ☐ **C** By train.
- ☐ **D** On a horse.

3 What did Scanlan do to check that McMurdo belonged to the Eminent Order of Freemen?
- ☐ **A** He touched his nose.
- ☐ **B** He winked.
- ☐ **C** He nodded.
- ☐ **D** He touched his eyebrow.

4 Where did the Scowrers live?
- ☐ **A** Chicago
- ☐ **B** Vermissa
- ☐ **C** London
- ☐ **D** Ireland

5 McMurdo found work...
- ☐ **A** at the lodge.
- ☐ **B** at McGinty's bar.
- ☐ **C** as a book-keeper.
- ☐ **D** at Shafter's house.

6 The man who was courting Ettie was called...
- ☐ **A** Scanlan.
- ☐ **B** McGinty.
- ☐ **C** Baldwin.
- ☐ **D** Shafter.

Grammar   **B2 FIRST**

2 **Look at the first sentence and complete the second sentence so that it has the same meaning as the first. Use between two and five words, including the word given.**

1 One of the men said he would show McMurdo the way to Shafter's house.

OFFERED

One of the men .... show McMurdo the way to Shafter's house.

2 McMurdo often showed that he was able to get angry very quickly.

ABILITY

McMurdo often showed ....
to get angry very quickly.

3 McMurdo thought that Shafter owed him an apology.

SHOULD

McMurdo thought that Shafter ....

4 The Scowrers always swear that their men were far from the scene
of the crime.

COMMITTED

The Scowrers always swear that their men were far from

....

Writing

3 **In this chapter, we have met some new characters. Write full
sentences to describe the ones below.**

1 Ettie: ....

....

2 Jack McMurdo: ....

....

3 Ted Baldwin: ....

....

Pre-Reading Activities • PART 2: Chapter 2

Listening

▶ 10 **4** **McMurdo finally visits Boss McGinty. Listen to the start of Chapter
2 and write a description of McGinty and his saloon.**

Boss McGinty: ....

....

McGinty's saloon: ....

....

PART 2:
THE SCOWRERS

Chapter 2
Bodymaster McGinty and Lodge 341 Vermissa

▶ 10 McGinty's saloon was crowded as usual, for it was the favourite place of the rougher men. The man was popular, but it was fear that made the people of the valley come to his bar. He was also a town councillor, elected by ruffians* who expected favours from him. Taxes were enormous, but public works weren't done, and decent citizens were afraid to say anything. So, Boss McGinty's saloon became bigger, and he became richer.

> A town councillor controlled everything that happened in the town. He was chosen by the townspeople in an election, but in these small towns, the councillors were often corrupt* and paid or forced people to vote for them.

McMurdo pushed open the swinging door and made his way through the crowds of men. The place was well-lit, with huge mirrors on every wall. There were several barmen, hard at work mixing* drinks. At the far end of the bar, stood a tall, strong, heavily-built man who could only be the famous McGinty himself. He had long black hair and a black beard, and the look of an honest man, but his dark eyes gave him a sinister, evil appearance. ⏹

▶ 11 McMurdo went up to McGinty and introduced himself. 'Councillor McGinty, I'm new here. Brother Scanlan of Lodge 341, Vermissa, advised me to come and see you.'

ruffian violent criminal, hooligan
corrupt dishonest
mix (here) put together different liquids to make a drink

McMurdo meets Boss McGinty.

68

'I'll have to look a bit closer into this Mr McMurdo,' said McGinty, taking McMurdo into a small room behind the bar. Then he sat on a barrel* and looked at him in silence for a few minutes.

Suddenly McGinty took out a revolver and said, 'If I thought you were playing any game on us, it would be dangerous for you.'

'This is a strange welcome for the Bodymaster of a lodge to give to a brother.'

'Yes, but you have to prove that,' said McGinty, and then he continued to ask McMurdo many questions about the lodge in Chicago.

'Why did you leave Chicago?' he asked.

'I can't tell you that!' answered McMurdo angrily.

'Then the truth is too bad to tell?'

'You can put it that way if you like.'

'See here, mister, you can't expect me, as Bodymaster, to allow into the lodge a man whose past I don't know.'

McMurdo took a worn newspaper cutting* from his pocket and said, 'You wouldn't say anything to the police, would you?'

McGinty reacted angrily to this question, so McMurdo apologised immediately and showed him the cutting, which reported the shooting of a man called Jonas Pinto in a saloon in Chicago the month before.

'Your work?' asked McGinty, as he handed back the paper.

McMurdo nodded.

'Why did you shoot him?'

'I was making false money and he was helping me to put them in circulation*, but things went bad, and I shot him and left the city.

In the 19th century the US government gave nearly 200 private banks permission to print their own notes and this made it easier for people to make false money.

barrel

cutting an article cut from a newspaper
in circulation (here) on the streets, to be used by the public

'Why did you come here, to the coal country?'

'I'd read in the papers that they weren't too particular in these parts.'

McGinty laughed. 'Can you still make those dollars?'

McMurdo took some from his pocket. McGinty held them to the light, then smiled.

'I can see no difference from the real dollar notes. I think you'll be a very useful brother! We need a bad man or two among us, Friend McMurdo, because there are times when we have to push back against those who are pushing us.'

'Well, I guess I'll be doing my part to push with the rest of the boys,' replied McMurdo, with a smile.

Just then, Ted Baldwin came rushing into the room. He looked furiously at McMurdo, then said, 'So, you got here first, did you? I've a word to say to you, Councillor, about this man!'

'Then say it here and now to my face,' cried McMurdo.

'I'll say it in my own time, and in my own way,' replied Baldwin.

'Tut! Tut!*' said McGinty, standing up. 'We mustn't greet a new brother in such a way, Baldwin. Hold out your hand, man, and make it up*!'

'Never!' cried Baldwin, angrily. 'I've offered to fight him if he thinks I've done anything wrong. Now, I'll leave it you, as Bodymaster, to decide what should be done.'

'What's the problem then?' asked McGinty.

'A young lady. She's free to choose for herself,' explained McMurdo.

'As it's between two brothers of the lodge I'd say that she is,' said the Boss.

---

tut tut sound made to show dislike or disapproval

make (it) up (here) settle their differences

'Is she?' cried Baldwin. 'That's your decision, is it? You would favour a stranger, instead of one that has stood by you for five years? You're not Bodymaster for life, Jack McGinty, so when it comes to the next vote—'

The Councillor sprang* at him like a tiger, but McMurdo stopped him.

'Maybe you think you could take my place as Bodymaster, Ted Baldwin!' shouted McGinty, angrily. 'But the lodge has to decide that, and while I am the Boss, no man will go against me or my decisions.'

'I have nothing against you,' mumbled* Baldwin.

'Well, then,' cried Boss McGinty, becoming jovial* again, 'we're all good friends again and that's the end of it.'

McMurdo held out his hand. Baldwin had to take it, for the Boss was looking at him. But he wasn't happy.

McGinty then invited McMurdo to Lodge 341 for the Saturday night meeting. 'We have our own ways and methods, different from Chicago,' he said. 'Come then and we'll make you a Freeman of the Vermissa Valley.'

The next day, McMurdo changed lodgings and Scanlan, his friend from the train, came to stay in the same place. However, Mr Shafter still allowed McMurdo to eat at his boarding house sometimes, so that he could still see Ettie. As weeks passed, the two of them grew even closer.

In his new lodgings, McMurdo felt safer making the false money. Some of the brothers, who had promised to keep the secret, often came to see him to get some of these notes, which were so perfect that nobody would notice they weren't real.

spring jump forwards quickly and suddenly   **jovial** jolly, happy
mumble speak in a quiet, unclear way

One night, when he was in the saloon, a new policeman came in and introduced himself to McGinty, who was behind the bar.

'You'll be the new captain?' said McGinty.

'That's so. We're looking to you, Councillor, and other leading citizens, to help us keep law and order in this town. Captain Marvin is my name.'

'We have our own town police, Captain Marvin,' said McGinty coldly. 'We don't need any officers from outside.'

'Well, we won't argue about that,' said the police officer, smiling. Then he saw Jack McMurdo.

'Hello!' he cried, looking him up and down. 'Here's an old friend!'

'I was never a friend to you, nor any other policeman,' said McMurdo.

'You're Jack McMurdo of Chicago, right enough*, and don't you deny it!'

McMurdo shook his head. 'I'm not denying it,' he said. 'Do you think I'm ashamed of my own name?'

'You should be,' replied Marvin. 'I was an officer in Chicago before I came here, and I know who you are. We haven't forgotten the shooting of Jonas Pinto up there.'

'I didn't shoot him,' replied McMurdo.

'Did you not? Well, I shouldn't really say it, but there was no clear case against you, and you're welcome to return to Chicago now.'

'I'm very well where I am, but I thank you for telling me.'

On Saturday night McMurdo was introduced to the lodge in Vermissa. Sixty lodge members met in a large room at the Union

The Vermissa town police were most likely controlled by Boss McGinty. The State police were probably sent to see what was happening in the town but couldn't do much about it.

---

right enough certainly, indeed

House. Bodymaster McGinty sat at the head of a long table with the higher lodge officials on either side. Ted Baldwin was among them. The members were mostly older men; but there were also young men from eighteen to twenty-five. It was difficult to believe that these honest-looking young men were, in truth, a dangerous gang of murderers. In ten long years, there had been no conviction* for their crimes. They had enough money to pay the best lawyers, nobody would testify* against them and they always had witnesses who would testify in their favour.

McMurdo knew that he would have <u>some ordeal</u> before him, but nobody would tell him what it was. He was taken outside the room so that the assembly* could decide. Before taking him back in, they rolled up his left shirt sleeve and tied a cord around the elbow. Then they put a hood over his head so that he could see nothing. When he was back in the assembly hall, he heard the voice of McGinty.

'John McMurdo,' said the voice, 'are you already a member of the Ancient Order of Freemen?'

He nodded his head. 'Is your lodge No. 29 Chicago?' Again, he nodded.

'Dark nights are unpleasant,' said the voice.

'Yes, for strangers to travel,' he answered.

'The clouds are heavy.'

'Yes, a storm is approaching.'

These words proved that he was indeed a Freeman. McGinty then asked him to prove his courage. He felt a terrible pain in his left arm, but he didn't shout out. When they took the hood from his head, he saw the sign of a circle with a triangle inside it, <u>branded on his</u>

Secret societies usually have official ceremonies to welcome new members. McMurdo knew that he would probably have to do something difficult and unpleasant to become a member of this unusual lodge and prove that he was loyal.

Although tattoos existed at this time, and had done so for centuries, this lodge preferred to use a more permanent and painful way of marking its members.

---

conviction being found guilty of a crime after a trial in court

testify to speak/give evidence in court

assembly (here) the group of people gathered there

arm. The other brothers lifted their sleeves to show the same sign. Then they all applauded* and congratulated him on becoming a new member of their lodge.

'One last word, Brother McMurdo,' said McGinty. 'You've already sworn the oath* of secrecy and fidelity*, and you know the punishment for any breach* of it is death. Do you accept the rule of the Bodymaster in all circumstances?'

'I do.'

'Then in the name of Lodge 341, Vermissa, I welcome you.'

The official lodge business then followed. McMurdo listened, with surprise, as they talked about the work of the brothers from this and other lodges in Vermissa Valley. They took money from the owners of small mining companies to protect them. Those that didn't pay or caused trouble were killed or driven out of the valley. The people in the valley were terrified to go against McGinty and his men. Then, a man called Morris suggested that they shouldn't drive out all the small mining bosses in the valley because big companies were coming in, which could be more dangerous to them. McGinty, however, said there was nothing to worry about.

'So long as the members of this lodge stand together, we will never be in danger. The big companies will pay us, just as the small companies do.' Suddenly raising his voice, he said, 'See here, Brother Morris, I have had my eye on you for some time! Be careful!'

Morris became pale as he fell back into his chair. He apologised to the Bodymaster, and swore that he was a faithful member of the lodge.

---

applaud to show approval by clapping
swear an oath to make a promise

fidelity faithfulness, loyalty
breach breaking a promise

Sir Arthur Conan Doyle

Finally, the Bodymaster read out a newspaper article in which the local editor*, James Stanger, criticised the lodge. The men were angry about this, but Morris, again, said that they shouldn't do anything because Stanger was an elderly man who was respected in the town. However, McGinty decided that Stanger should be hurt, but not killed, to teach him a lesson.

Late that evening, Ted Baldwin and some young men, including McMurdo, went to Stanger's office. The men hit him with sticks and were about to kill the poor man, but McMurdo stopped them and reminded them that McGinty had said he shouldn't be killed. Baldwin looked at him in amazement and cried, 'Who are you to interfere? You are new to the lodge. Stand back!' He raised his stick, but McMurdo had pulled his pistol* out of his pocket.

'Stand back yourself!' he cried. 'I'll shoot you in the face if you lay a hand on me.'

Then they heard shouting in the street, so they left the poor editor and ran outside and along to the Union House. Some went to McGinty's saloon, and whispered to the Boss that the job had been done. Others, and among them McMurdo, ran to their own homes.

Next morning, McMurdo read about the attack on the editor in the Herald newspaper. Mr Stanger, who was badly injured, had recognised some of the men and accused the Scowrers. There was a knock at his door and his landlady* gave him a letter. It was unsigned but the handwriting was that of a well-educated man. It asked him to go to Miller Hill immediately, as this person had something very

It is ironic that Baldwin's death in Birlstone Manor was caused by being shot in the face.

editor the person responsible for the contents of a newspaper
pistol gun

landlady woman who owns a boarding house

76

important to tell him. At first, he hesitated as it was a public park in the town centre, but in the winter it was deserted*, so he decided to go and find out who had sent the message.

When McMurdo arrived, he saw a man with his hat pulled down and the collar of his coat up. When he turned his face, he saw that it was Brother Morris.

'I wanted to speak to you, Mr McMurdo,' said the older man, speaking with hesitation.

'Why didn't you sign the letter?'

'One has to be cautious, mister. You never know who to trust.'

'Surely one may trust brothers of the lodge.'

'No, no, not always,' cried Morris. 'Whatever we say, or even think, seems to go back to McGinty.'

'Look here!' said McMurdo sternly*. 'It was only last night, as you know well, that I swore good faith* to our Bodymaster. Are you asking me to break my oath?'

'If that's what you think,' said Morris sadly, 'I can only say that I'm sorry I gave you the trouble to come and meet me. Things are bad when two free citizens cannot speak to each other.'

McMurdo, who had been watching his companion very carefully, relaxed a little. 'I'm new, as you know, Mr Morris,' he said, 'but I'll listen to what you have to say.'

'And then tell Boss McGinty!' said Morris bitterly.

'No, you are wrong,' cried McMurdo. 'I am loyal to the lodge, but I would never repeat to any other what you might say to me in confidence.'

McMurdo doesn't know Morris so he has to tell him he is loyal to the lodge in case he himself talks to McGinty about the secret meeting. However, he also wants Morris to know that he is an honest man and would never betray him.

---

deserted empty of people
sternly in a very serious way

faith loyalty, trust

'I may be putting my very life in your hands by what I say, but as you are new, I thought your conscience* cannot yet be as hardened as theirs. That's why I decided to speak to you. I want to ask you, when you joined the Freeman's society in Chicago and swore vows* of charity and fidelity, did you ever think that it would lead you to crime?'

'If you call it crime,' McMurdo answered.

'Call it crime!' cried Morris, his voice vibrating* with passion. 'Last night, a man old enough to be your father was beaten almost to death. Was that not a crime?'

'There are some would say it was war,' said McMurdo, 'a war of two classes.'

'Well, did you think of such a thing when you joined the Freeman's society in Chicago?'

'No, I have to say, I did not.'

'Nor did I when I joined it in Philadelphia. It was just a club. Then I heard of this place and I came to better myself. So I thought! My wife and three children came with me. I opened a store on Market Square, and I did well. They heard I was a Freeman, and I was forced to join the local lodge. I found that I was under the orders of an evil criminal and caught in a network of crime. What could I do? Every word I said to make things better was taken as treason*, same as it was last night. I can't get away. If I leave the society, I know well that it means murder for me, and maybe even my wife and children. Oh, man, it is awful—awful!' He put his hands to his face, and his body shook as he cried.

This is another reference to the Union problems at that time when the rich factory and mine owners were against the poor working class.

---

conscience a moral sense of right or wrong
vow promise, oath

vibrate to shake
treason betraying someone

'You were too soft for the job,' said McMurdo. 'You're the wrong sort for such work.'

'I had a conscience and a religion, but they made me a criminal among them. I was chosen for a job. If I'd refused to do it, I knew well what would have happened to me. Maybe I'm a coward. Anyway, I went, and it will probably haunt me forever. I nearly fainted with the horror of it, and yet I had to keep a smiling face. But I was a criminal. I'm a good Catholic, but the priest would have nothing to do with me when he heard I was a Scowrer. Are you ready to be a cold-blooded* murderer also, or can we do anything to stop it? This is the Valley of Fear, the Valley of Death. The terror is in the hearts of the people from dusk* to dawn. Wait and you will learn for yourself.'

'Well, I'll let you know what I think when I have seen more,' said McMurdo carelessly. 'It's clear that you're not the man for the place. The sooner you sell your business, the better it will be for you. What you have said is safe with me, but if I thought you were an informer...'

'No, no!' cried Morris.

'Well, let's leave it at that. I'll think about what you have said. I expect you meant kindly by speaking to me like this. Now I have to go home.'

'One word before you go,' said Morris. 'If we've been seen together, they may want to know what we've spoken about.'

'Ah! Yes, of course.'

'I offered you a job in my store.'

'And I refused it. That's our business. Well, goodbye, Brother Morris. I hope things will be better with you in the future.'

Morris is warning that McMurdo will be forced to do violent things for the Scowrers as he was. He is the first one to refer to this place as The Valley of Fear, something repeated only by good people in the town. He hopes McMurdo can help stop the Scowrers.

---

cold-blooded behaving in a very cruel or violent way

dusk sunset

That same afternoon, McGinty came to visit McMurdo. He sat down opposite the young man and looked at him steadily for some time, a look which was as steadily returned.

'I don't usually visit people, Brother McMurdo,' he said at last. 'But I thought I'd come and see you in your own house.'

'I'm proud to see you here, Councillor,' McMurdo answered. 'I didn't expect such an honour.'

'What were you speaking to Brother Morris about on Miller Hill this morning?'

The question came so suddenly that it was a good thing that he had his answer prepared. He laughed and said, 'Morris didn't know I could earn a living here at home -and he won't know either. But he's a good-hearted old chap. He thought he'd do me a favour by offering me a job in his store.'

'And you refused it?'

'Of course. Couldn't I earn ten times as much in my own bedroom with four hours' work?'

McGinty agreed. Then he advised McMurdo not to be too friendly with Morris. When he asked why, McGinty just said because he told him so.

'Did Morris say anything to you against the lodge – or me?'

'No.'

'Well, that's because he doesn't trust you. But, in his heart, he's not a loyal brother. We know that well. So, we watch him and wait for the time to punish him. But if you're friendly with a disloyal man, we might think that you were disloyal, too. See?'

This is proof that Boss McGinty has spies* everywhere and really does know everything that goes on in the town.

Here, McMurdo is talking about the false notes he can make in his own home.

spy undercover agent who secretly gets information for an organisation

'I'd like to know,' said McMurdo, 'how you heard that I'd spoken with Morris at all?'

McGinty laughed. 'It's my business to know what goes on in this town,' he said. 'I hear about everything that happens.'

Suddenly, as McGinty was about to leave, three policemen burst through the door. McMurdo sprang to his feet and was about to pull out his revolver, but he stopped as he realised that two rifles were pointed at his head. Captain Marvin, came into the room. He smiled at McMurdo.

'I thought you'd be getting into trouble, Mr Crooked McMurdo of Chicago,' he said. 'Take your hat and come along with us.'

'What am I accused of?' asked McMurdo.

'The attack on old Editor Stanger at the Herald office.'

'Well, if that's all you have against him,' cried McGinty with a laugh, 'you can save yourself a lot of trouble. This man was with me in my saloon till midnight, and a dozen men can prove it.'

At the police station, McMurdo found Baldwin and three other criminals from the night before. However, as Freemen, they had nothing to worry about. The next day, the judge decided that there wasn't enough evidence to convict* them. Mr Stanger couldn't say who had attacked him and the men were allowed to go free. In the court, brothers of the lodge applauded but there were others who were angry.

After being arrested and judged innocent, Jack McMurdo was even more popular at the lodge. However, Mr Shafter wouldn't allow him to

After Mr Stanger had said he was attacked by the Scowrers, he was probably too afraid to identify the men responsible. The men from the lodge would also have been paid to say that the ones who were responsible, were in the saloon at the time. So, there was no evidence.

---

convict to find someone guilty of a crime

enter his house. Ettie was in love with Jack, but her own good sense told her she couldn't marry a criminal. One morning, she decided to try, possibly for the last time, to convince him to stay away from those evil influences. She went to his house and found him in his sitting-room. He was sitting at a table, with his back turned and a letter in front of him. She crept up* quietly behind him to surprise him. But, like a tiger, he turned on her. At the same time, he crumpled up* the paper that lay before him.

'It's you!' he said, in amazement. 'I'm so sorry, my darling.' But Ettie saw guilt and fear in his face.

'What's wrong, Jack?' she cried. 'Why were you so scared of me?'

She was suddenly suspicious and thought he was writing a letter to another woman.

'Were you writing to your wife?' she cried.

'I'm not married, Ettie! You're the only woman on earth for me. I swear it! It's lodge business and secret, even to you. So, don't worry!' She felt that he was telling the truth.

'But how can I not worry, Jack, when I know that you are one of the Scowrers? Please, Jack! Give it up!'

'Sure, my darling. Even if I wanted to, how could I do it? Do you think that the lodge would let a man go free with all its secrets?'

'I've thought of that, Jack. Father has saved some money and he's ready to go. We could run away together to Philadelphia or New York, where we would be safe from them.'

McMurdo laughed. 'Do you not think the lodge could find us there?'

'Well, then, anywhere to get away from this Valley of Fear!'

Jack has a secret that he can't talk to Ettie about, so she thinks that he has to do dangerous work for the Scowrers.

creep up (behind someone) to surprise someone and move closer to them without being seen or heard

crumple up to roll into a ball

McMurdo thought of old Brother Morris. 'That's the second time I've heard the valley called that,' he said. 'I can't leave here yet. Let me find a way of getting out of it honourably.'

'There is no honour in such a matter,' said Ettie, sadly.

'Well, it's just how you look at it. But if you give me six months, a year at the latest, I'll make sure that we can leave the valley.'

Ettie returned to her father's house much happier than she had ever been since Jack McMurdo had come into her life.

McMurdo thought that, as a member, he would know all the lodge business; but he soon discovered that the organisation was more complex*. Even Boss McGinty didn't know everything, because there was an official, living at Hobson's Patch, with power over several different lodges. McMurdo had only seen him once: a sly*, grey-haired, evil-looking little man called Evans Pott, who even the great Boss of Vermissa feared.

One day, Scanlan received a note from Boss McGinty, which informed him that Evans Pott was sending two men to do a job in the neighbourhood and asked if the strangers could stay with McMurdo and Scanlan for a few days. The men were friendly but wouldn't talk about the job they were there to do. One morning, when McMurdo and Scanlan heard the men going out early, they followed them. They headed outside the town, with their hats pulled down and their collars up to hide their faces, to a big mining company run by Josiah H. Dunn. When the young mine manager and the company engineer came out of the office, they immediately shot them both and, to

McMurdo is a good man but he's in a situation that will be difficult to get out of.

This violent and criminal organisation was not just in Vermissa. It included other lodges around Vermissa Valley and the members would do favours for those in other lodges when they were needed. This usually involved dealing with something in a violent way.

complex not simple, complicated   **sly** clever, tricky (like a fox)

83

frighten the miners waiting there to go down the mine, they shot into the air above their heads.

There were great celebrations at the Union House that night. Ted Baldwin and other men from Vermissa had also done a job in another district. It had been a great day for the Scowrers. Boss McGinty called McMurdo over.

'See here, my lad,' said he, 'I've got a job for you at last. Take two men with you. We have to deal with Chester Wilcox, the chief foreman* of the Iron Dike Company. He's a hard man to get. At night, he's home with his wife, three children, and a maid. If you could blow up* his house—'

'There are these two women and the children. Do they go up too? They've done nothing.'

'Are you refusing to do it?' asked McGinty, abruptly.

'No, Councillor! Do you think I'd refuse to follow an order from the Bodymaster of my own lodge? Give me a night or two to see the house and make my plans.'

'Very good,' said McGinty, shaking him by the hand. 'I leave it with you.'

Two nights later, McMurdo and two young men went to blow up the Wilcox house. But it had been for nothing! Chester Wilcox and his family had moved only the day before to a safe place.

'Leave him to me,' said McMurdo. 'I'll get him if I have to wait a year for him.'

It was reported, a few weeks later, that Wilcox had been shot.

---

foreman a man responsible for a group of workers

blow up (here) to make something explode

This was how the Society of Freemen and the deeds* of the Scowrers, for a long time, spread fear in the district. Many innocent men, women and families were killed. It all happened in the same terrible winter. The shadow lay darkly upon the Valley of Fear. In the spring, the trees blossomed*, and there was hope for the future, but not for the men and women who lived in terror. The cloud above them had never been so dark and hopeless as in the early summer of the year 1875. ⬛

There seemed to be no hope for the innocent people who lived in Vermissa Valley. They were in an impossible situation that was difficult to get out of.

deed an action

blossom to bloom, have flowers or new leaves

Reading **B2 FIRST**

1 **Read the following paragraph. Six phrases have been removed. Choose one phrase from A to G to fit in each gap (1-6). There is one extra that has not been used.**

A His hat was pulled down and the collar of his coat was hiding his face.
B He said that he was loyal to the lodge.
C At first, he hesitated.
D He trusted Morris.
E He said that McGinty and the Scowrers were dangerous.
F He said he'd been afraid to sign the letter.
G His landlady gave him a letter.

On Sunday morning, there was a knock at McMurdo's door. **(1)** ....
It was unsigned but the handwriting was that of a well-educated man. It asked him to go to Miller Hill immediately, as this person had something very important to tell him. **(2)** .... It was a public park in the town centre, but in the winter it was deserted, so he decided to go and find out who had sent the message. When McMurdo arrived, he saw a man there. **(3)** .... It was Brother Morris. The older man said that he wanted to speak to McMurdo in private. **(4)** .... He didn't know who he could trust, especially at the lodge. McMurdo was surprised to hear this but he said he would listen to what Morris had to say. **(5)** .... However, he promised that he would not repeat anything he was told in confidence, to McGinty or anyone else at the lodge. Morris said that he hated living in Vermissa. When he'd arrived there, he had been forced to join the lodge. **(6)** ....
The people of Vermissa were living in the Valley of Fear.

Grammar **B2 FIRST**

2 **Read the text and use the words on the right to make a word that fits the gap on the same line.**

After McMurdo spoke to Morris, Boss McGinty came to visit McMurdo.
He didn't often visit **(1)** .... in their homes.   **PERSON**
He sat down in a chair opposite the **(2)** ....   **YOUTH**
man and looked at him **(3)** .... for some time.   **STEADY**
McMurdo was surprised but he told McGinty that he felt

(4) .... that he had visited him. Then, all of a **(5)** .... , McGinty told him that he knew about the **(6)** .... with Morris, and warned him that he shouldn't get too friendly with him. He thought that Morris was being **(7)** .... to the lodge, and he told McMurdo that any kind of **(8)** .... with him might show he too wasn't loyal. McMurdo was really surprised that McGinty knew he had spoken to Morris in the park. He realised that Morris had been telling the **(9)** .... McGinty knew everything that was going on in the town. He was glad that he had prepared an excuse.

He said that Morris had offered him a job in his shop but he'd told him that **(10)** .... he had to refuse.

PRIDE
SUDDENLY
MEET

LOYALTY

FRIEND

TRUE

FORTUNE

Writing

3 In the next chapter, the Scowrers discover that a detective called Pinky Edwards is investigating them. Choose an adjective from the box below, to describe how you think the following characters will react to the news.

> frightened - worried - decisive

1

Boss McGinty will be ....

2

Jack McMurdo will be ....

3

Mr Morris will be ....

Speaking

4 The lodge members have a meeting to discuss what to do about the detective. What do you think they will decide to do? What do you think will happen to the Scowrers? Discuss with a partner.

PART 2:
THE SCOWRERS

Chapter 3
Birdy Edwards

▶ 12 It was the height of the reign of terror. McMurdo had been promoted*
and was certain to become Bodymaster one day, when McGinty
retired. He was even more popular with the other Freemen, except
Ted Baldwin of course, but hated by the people of Vermissa. In spite
of* their terror, the citizens were gathering together against the lodge
members. Rumours had reached the lodge of secret gatherings in
the Herald office and of the distribution of weapons among the law-
abiding* people. But McGinty and his men were not worried. They
were numerous, powerful and well-armed. As had happened in the
past, if they were arrested, nothing would happen to them.

One Saturday evening in May, when McMurdo was leaving his house
to go to the lodge meeting, Morris, the weaker brother of the order,
came to see him. He didn't look well.

'Can I speak with you freely, Mr McMurdo?'

'Sure.'

'I can't forget that I spoke to you once, and that you kept it to
yourself, even though the Boss himself came to ask you about it.'

'What else could I do if you trusted me? But, I didn't agree with
what you said.'

The townspeople were trying to protect themselves from the Scowrers, but even when Boss McGinty heard this, he thought that he and his men were too powerful and could never be forced out*.

---

be promoted to get a better job or position
in spite of despite

law-abiding obedient to the laws of society
forced out made to leave

'I know that. But you're the only one I can speak to and be safe. I have a secret and if I tell it, it will mean murder, for sure. If I don't, it may bring the end of us all, I'm so worried. I just don't know what to do!'

McMurdo looked at the man seriously. His body was trembling. 'Let me hear it,' he said.

'I can tell it to you all in one sentence,' said Morris. 'There's a detective investigating us.'

McMurdo stared at him in astonishment. 'You're crazy,' he said. 'The place is full of police and detectives and they've never harmed us.'

'No, no, it's no man of the district. Have you ever heard of Pinkerton's?'

'I've read about them.'

'Well, you can take it from me, they always get their man. If a Pinkerton man is involved in this business, we'll all be destroyed.'

'We must kill him,' said McMurdo immediately.

'Ah, it's the first thought that came to you! But I don't want a man to be murdered. And yet it's our own lives that may be in danger. What shall I do?'

McMurdo shared the other's opinion about the danger, and that something had to be done about it. He gripped* Morris's shoulders and shook him.

'See here, man,' he cried, 'you won't gain* anything by crying like an old woman. Let's have the facts. Who is he? Where is he? How did you hear of him? Why did you come to me?'

The Pinkerton National Detective Agency was founded in Chicago, USA, in 1850, by a Scottish immigrant called Allan Pinkerton. By the end of the 19th century it was the largest private detective organisation in the world. Historically, its main work was with problems in unions, and they used spies in various organisations when working for big companies and the US government. It still exists today, as part of a Swedish security company.

grip to hold tightly   **gain** (here) solve

'I came to you because I know that you are the only man who can advise me.'

He handed McMurdo a letter. 'I received a letter from an old friend in the East, asking me how the Scowrers were getting on here. He told me that the rich owners of the railroad* company and other corporations had employed Pinkertons to investigate them and that their best detective, Birdy Edwards, was on the case.'

McMurdo read the letter then stayed silent for some time. Like Morris, his friend's words worried him.

'Does anyone else know of this?' he asked.

'I have told no one else.'

'But this man—your friend—would he be likely to write to any other person of the lodge?' asked McMurdo, looking worried.

'It's likely enough. I think he knows a few of the lodge members.'

'I was asking because he may have given some description of this man Birdy Edwards—then we could find him.'

'Well, it's possible. But I don't think he knows him. He is just telling me the news that he has heard. How would he know this Pinkerton man?' asked Morris.

McMurdo promised Morris that he would deal with it and leave his name out of it.

'I will say that I received the letter. Don't worry about anything. We'll deal with this man Pinkerton and make him sorry for trying to destroy us.'

'You wouldn't kill this man?' asked Morris. 'I feel that his blood is on my hands!'

---

railroad what trains travel along

Morris shows
McMurdo a letter.

'Self-protection is no murder,' said McMurdo seriously, but it was clear that he didn't believe this. He knew that danger was coming and he had to prepare for the worst.

On his way to the lodge, McMurdo stopped at Shafter's boarding house. He wasn't allowed to enter, but when he tapped* at the window Ettie came out to him. She could see fear in his face.

'Something has happened!' she cried. 'Oh, Jack, you're in danger!'

'Yes, but it's not very bad, my darling. Still, it may be wise for us to make a move before it gets worse.'

'Make a move?'

After reading the letter, McMurdo sees there's going to be trouble and he wants Ettie and her father to be safe.

'I promised you once that I would go some day. I think the time is coming. I had news tonight, bad news, and I see trouble coming. You said you would come with me if I went'

'Oh, Jack, of course I would!'

'Would you trust me?' asked McMurdo.

She put her hand in his without a word.

'Well, then, listen to what I say, and do as I order you, for it's the only way for us. Things are going to happen in this valley. If I go, by day or night, you must come with me. Will you come?' asked McMurdo.

'Yes, Jack, I'll come.'

'When you get my message, come immediately to the waiting room at the station and stay there till I come for you.'

Now that he had begun his own preparations for escape, McMurdo went to the lodge. The meeting had already started. He raised his hand to interrupt the discussions.

tap to knock lightly

'Eminent Bodymaster and Brothers,' he said in a serious voice. 'I have something important to tell you.' He took the letter from his pocket.

'I have bad news about something that could destroy us all. There is a Pinkerton detective called Birdy Edwards, who is working in the valley to collect evidence that could send many of us here to prison.'

There was a dead silence in the room. Then the chairman asked, 'What is your evidence for this, Brother McMurdo?'

'It's in this letter which I have received,' said McMurdo, and he read the letter aloud.

'Let me say, Mr Chairman,' said one of the older brothers, 'that I've heard of Birdy Edwards, and that he has the name of being the best man in the Pinkerton service.'

'Does anyone know him by sight?' asked McGinty.

'Yes,' said McMurdo, 'I do.'

There was a murmur* of astonishment through the hall.

'If we act quickly and wisely,' he continued. 'we'll have nothing to fear.'

'What do we have to fear, anyway? What can he know about our business?' asked McGinty.

'There may be weaker brothers in our lodges, Councillor, that could be paid for our secrets. Maybe he's got them already. There's only one solution,' said McMurdo. 'I think this is too important to discuss with all the members. I suggest that a small group of us meet in private to discuss what should be done.'

The meeting finished early and when the other brothers had left, McGinty, Baldwin and five others asked McMurdo what he knew.

Even after hearing that the Scowrers are being investigated by a Pinkerton agent, Boss McGinty is so arrogant that he thinks he can't be touched.

murmur people talking in low voices

'I've met Birdy Edwards,' McMurdo explained. 'He's using the name of Steve Wilson, and he's staying at Hobson's Patch.'

'How do you know this?'

'Because I met him on the train on Wednesday. It was only when I read this letter that I thought he could be the man. He said he was a reporter. He wanted to know about the Scowrers for a New York newspaper. He said he'd pay well for any information, so I told him some things that weren't important, and he gave me twenty dollars. He said he'd give me a lot more for other information.'

'How do you know he isn't a newspaper reporter?' asked McGinty.

'When we got off at Hobson's Patch, he went to the telegraph* office. So, after he left, I went in and spoke to the operator. He told me that this Steve Wilson sent off telegrams to his office every day in a strange code. He thought perhaps it was because it was special news for his newspaper. That's what I thought too at the time, but now I think differently.'

'Why not go right now and fix him,' someone suggested.

'I'd go immediately, if I knew where to find him,' said McMurdo. 'I'll find out from the telegraph operator tomorrow morning, and then I'll go and see him. I'll offer him all the secrets of the lodge for a price and say that he should come to my house for the papers. It's quiet there late in the evening when nobody is about. Then, you can do the rest.' ▪

---

telegraph an old way of sending long-distance messages

McMurdo tells the Brothers about Birdy Edwards.

Reading   **B2 FIRST**

1 **Read Chapter 3 again and choose the correct answer A, B, C or D.**

1 When Mr Morris received the letter about the Pinkerton detective, he...
- ☐ **A** sent a reply to his friend.
- ☐ **B** was afraid and hid it.
- ☐ **C** told Jack McMurdo about it.
- ☐ **D** took it to Boss McGinty at the Lodge.

2 Who was the only person that Morris trusted?
- ☐ **A** Jack McGinty
- ☐ **B** Jack McMurdo
- ☐ **C** Ted Baldwin
- ☐ **D** Birdy Edwards

3 Who had employed the Pinkerton detective to investigate the Scowrers?
- ☐ **A** Mr Morris's friend
- ☐ **B** The railroad company
- ☐ **C** A member of the lodge
- ☐ **D** The government

4 Where did McMurdo go after he spoke to Morris?
- ☐ **A** To his apartment
- ☐ **B** To Ettie's house
- ☐ **C** To the lodge
- ☐ **D** To the train station

5 McMurdo told the lodge members that...
- ☐ **A** he didn't know Birdy Edwards.
- ☐ **B** he'd seen Birdy Edwards at the police station.
- ☐ **C** Birdy Edwards was really a reporter.
- ☐ **D** Birdy Edwards had paid him for information.

6 When did McMurdo want to meet Birdy Edwards at his house?
- ☐ **A** The next evening
- ☐ **B** That same evening
- ☐ **C** The next morning
- ☐ **D** The following afternoon

Vocabulary

2 **Write the comparatives and superlatives of the following adjectives.**

1 popular   ....   the ....
2 weak   ....   the ....
3 good   ....   the ....
4 bad   ....   the ....
5 crazy   ....   the ....

Grammar

3 **Choose the correct preposition (A, B, C or D).**

When Mr Morris spoke to McMurdo, he was trembling **(1)** ....
fear. He took a letter **(2)** .... his pocket and showed it to
McMurdo, who stared at it **(3)** .... amazement. Morris had
received it from an old friend **(4)** .... the east. It said that the
Scowrers were being investigated **(5)** .... a detective from the
Pinkerton Agency, and their best detective was **(6)** .... the
case. McMurdo sat in silence **(7)** .... a short time, and then he
told Morris that he would deal **(8)** .... it.

1	**A** in	**B** with	**C** for	**D** about
2	**A** in	**B** to	**C** from	**D** on
3	**A** with	**B** in	**C** from	**D** at
4	**A** on	**B** at	**C** to	**D** in
5	**A** from	**B** about	**C** by	**D** for
6	**A** on	**B** in	**C** at	**D** for
7	**A** about	**B** for	**C** in	**D** at
8	**A** to	**B** in	**C** for	**D** with

Pre-Reading Activities • PART 2: Chapter 4

Listening

▶ 13 **4** **Listen to the start of the next chapter and fill in the spaces in the text.**

McMurdo went to Hobson's Patch as agreed. He **(1)** ....
and saw McGinty at the Union House. 'He's coming,' he said. 'Good!' said
McGinty. The Boss had become **(2)** .... and powerful man
and the thought of **(3)** .... seemed even more terrible for him.
'Do you think he knows much?' he asked anxiously. McMurdo shook his
head. 'He's been here some time—**(4)** .... at least. If he's been
working among us all that time, I expect he has got results, and that he's
passed them on.' 'Did he seem to suspect a trap?' McMurdo laughed and
took out a bundle of **(5)** .... 'I think he'd do anything to get
information about the Scowrers, and he'll give me much more when he has
seen **(6)** ....' 'Didn't he ask you **(7)** .... bring him
the papers?' 'Obviously he knows I wouldn't carry such things!' McMurdo
then explained to McGinty how they should **(8)** .... in his
room and deal with him.

Chapter 4

The Trap

▶ 13 McMurdo went to Hobson's Patch as agreed. He returned in the afternoon and saw McGinty at the Union House.

'He's coming,' he said.

'Good!' said McGinty. The Boss had become a very rich and powerful man, and the thought of going to prison seemed even more terrible for him.

'Do you think he knows much?' he asked anxiously.

McMurdo shook his head. 'He's been here some time—six weeks at least. If he's been working among us all that time, I expect he has got results, and that he's passed them on.'

'Did he seem to suspect a trap?'

McMurdo laughed and took out a bundle of dollar notes. 'I think he'd do anything to get information about the Scowrers, and he'll give me much more when he has seen all my papers.'

'Didn't he ask you why you didn't bring him the papers?'

'Obviously he knows I wouldn't carry such things!'

McMurdo then explained to McGinty how they should trap the detective in his room and deal with him. ■

Boss McGinty has obviously had time to think about the situation and realises that, if other people have spoken to the detective, he could be arrested and sent to prison. He is only thinking about himself.

14 'This is how we should do it. You'll all wait in the big room. I'll take him into the other room, and leave him there while I get the papers. That will give me the chance to tell you how things are going. Then I'll go back to him with some false papers. While he's reading them, I'll grab his arms. You'll hear me call and you'll rush in quickly. I can hold him till you come.'

'It's a good plan,' said McGinty. 'The lodge will owe you a debt for this.'

When he returned home, he made his own preparations. He looked around the room in which the detective was to be trapped. It was large with a long table in the centre. On one side there were windows with just light curtains.

Finally, he spoke to Scanlan. He was a Scowrer, but he was weak, and he was secretly horrified* by the actions he had sometimes been forced to take part in. McMurdo told him what was going to happen and told him to stay away that night.

Scanlan was probably like many of the Scowrers who had been good men, forced to do violent acts out of fear.

The men came, as arranged, and McMurdo took them into the room to wait for the detective to arrive. There were three knocks at the door.

'Quiet!' said McMurdo, and he left the room, closing the door behind him. They heard McMurdo walking down the corridor, then voices and a door closing. They waited for McMurdo to call them. Instead, he came in and looked at them seriously, as they sat around the table.

horrified very shocked, filled with horror

'Well!' cried Boss McGinty at last. 'Is he here? Is Birdy Edwards here?'

'Yes,' McMurdo answered slowly. 'Birdy Edwards is here. I am Birdy Edwards!'

For ten seconds there was complete silence. Then, suddenly, rifles were fired through each window, tearing the curtains. Boss McGinty dived towards the half-opened door, but Captain Marvin was waiting there with a revolver in his hand. The Boss stepped back and fell into his chair.

'You're safer there, Councillor,' said the man they had known as McMurdo. 'And you, Baldwin, put your gun away. There are forty armed men round this house. You have no chance. Take their pistols, Marvin!'

'I'd like to say a word to you before we separate,' said the man who had trapped them. 'At last I can tell you the truth. I'm Birdy Edwards of Pinkerton's. I was chosen to break up your gang. Only Captain Marvin and my employers knew about it. But it's over tonight, and I am the winner!'

The seven pale, rigid* faces looked up at him, with hatred in their eyes.

'When they gave me this job, I didn't believe there was a society like yours. They told me it was to do with the Freemen; so, I went to Chicago and became one. I found no harm in the society, but a lot of good. When I came here, I learned I was wrong, so I stayed to do my job. I had to pretend the police were after me. I joined your lodge,

Birdy Edwards' character was based on a real Pinkerton detective who spied on the Molly Maguires, a 19th century secret and violent organisation of mainly Irish-American coal miners.

rigid hard, tight

100

and maybe they'll say that I was as bad as you. At least I stopped you, Baldwin, from killing old man Stanger. And I warned Chester Wilcox that we were going to blow his house up. I couldn't save everyone but I'll see that you're all punished for your actions.'

'You traitor*!' hissed* McGinty through closed teeth.

'Yes, you may call me that, but there are many that would call me their saviour*. If I hadn't heard that my secret was coming out, I'd have stayed longer. Now, Marvin, take them away.'

There is little more to tell. Scanlan had been given a sealed* note to take to Miss Ettie Shafter, and early in the morning, she and her father boarded a special train to Chicago, sent by the railroad company. Ten days later, Jack and Ettie were married.

McGinty and his men were convicted for their terrible crimes. At last, the cloud was lifted forever from the valley. The work of Birdy Edwards was complete. However, after ten years, Ted Baldwin and others would be out of prison and free to get revenge on McMurdo. They tried to kill him twice in Chicago, so he changed his name to Douglas and moved to California. When poor Ettie died, and he heard that Baldwin was on his track once again, he decided to move to England, where he married again and lived as John Douglas for five years, which ended with the strange happenings we have heard about. ◉

Thinking back to previous chapters, it seems obvious now that he had deliberately stopped the killing of Mr Stanger and the Wilcox family. But he couldn't stop the Scowrers from killing everyone, or his secret would have been discovered.

---

traitor a person who betrays someone or something
hiss to make a sharp 's' sound

saviour someone who saves another person's life
sealed closed with something to stop others opening it

Epilogue

15 In the case of John Douglas, the judge decided that he had acted in self-defence, and so was allowed to go free.

A legal term that means that if you kill someone who was trying to harm you, you will not be found guilty and sent to prison.

'Get him out of England at any cost,' wrote Holmes to the wife. 'It is still too dangerous for your husband here in England.'

Two months had gone by, and we'd almost forgotten about the case. Then one morning Holmes received a strange letter. It said, 'Dear me, Mr Holmes. Dear me!' and there was no signature. I laughed, but Holmes looked very serious.

Last night, Cecil Barker, our friend from the Manor House came to see Holmes.

'I've had bad news—terrible news, Mr Holmes,' he said.

'I feared that,' said Holmes.

'You've not had a message, have you?'

'I've had a note from someone who has.'

'It's poor Douglas. They tell me his name is Edwards, but he'll always be Jack Douglas to me. He and Mrs Douglas left for South Africa three weeks ago. The ship reached Cape Town last night. I received this message from Mrs Douglas this morning to say that Jack has been lost overboard*. No one knows how the accident happened.'

overboard falling into the sea from a ship

'Well, I've no doubt that it was no accident.'

'Those evil Scowrers—'

'No, my good sir,' said Holmes. 'There's a master hand here. This is the work of Moriarty.'

'How does this man have anything to do with it?'

'I can only say that we first heard about this business from one of his men. These Americans, having an English job to do, asked this great consultant in crime. I warned Mr Douglas that he was still in danger.'

'Are you telling me that we have to accept this?' said Barker angrily.

'No, I'm not saying that,' said Holmes, and he seemed to be looking far into the future. 'I'm not saying that he can't be beaten. But you must give me time—you must give me time!' ■

Ted Baldwin and the Scowrers had needed help in England to get to John Douglas/Jack McMurdo and had paid Prof. Moriarty to do it.

Sherlock Holmes is sure that he will eventually get the proof to convict Prof. Moriarty.

Reading

1 Decide if the following sentences are True (T) or False (F).

		T	F
1	McMurdo said he would take Birdy Edwards into the big room.	☐	☐
2	McMurdo told Scanlan what he was planning to do.	☐	☐
3	Boss McGinty was really Birdy Edwards.	☐	☐
4	The house was surrounded by Scowrers.	☐	☐
5	Captain Marvin knew who Birdy Edwards really was.	☐	☐
6	Jack and Ettie got married in Chicago.	☐	☐
7	Ettie died in England ten years later.	☐	☐
8	Ted Baldwin changed his name to John Douglas	☐	☐

Grammar **B2 FIRST**

2 Look at the first sentence and complete the second sentence so that it has the same meaning as the first. Use between two and five words, including the word given.

1 McMurdo said he'd come back to tell McGinty how things were going.
   LET
   McMurdo said he'd come back to .... how things were going.

2 Scanlan was horrified by the actions he had been forced to take part in.
   MADE
   Scanlan was horrified by the actions .... take part in.

3 If McMurdo hadn't heard that his secret was coming out, he'd have stayed longer.
   ABOUT
   If McMurdo hadn't heard that his secret was ...., he'd have stayed longer.

4 Cecil Barker was sure that John Douglas had been killed.
   DOUBT
   Cecil Barker .... that John Douglas had been killed.

Crossword

3 **Read the clues and complete the crossword.**

Clues

1 Shocked

2

3

4 The judge's decision (2 words)

5 Fake, not real

6

7 Person who investigates crimes

8

9

10 To allow, let

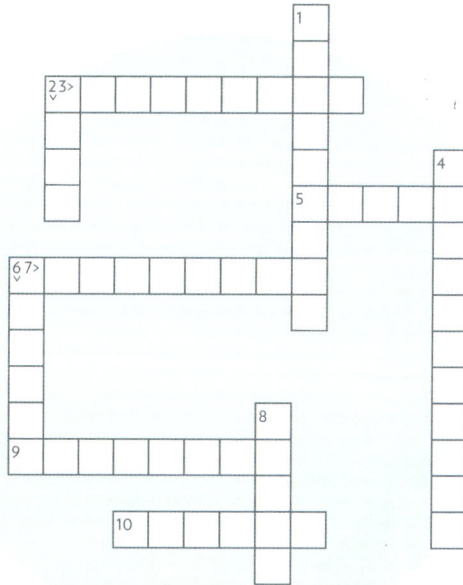

Speaking

4 **In the Epilogue in Chapter 4, we find out the judge's verdict. Do you agree with the judge's decision? What facts do you think he considered when he was deciding what should happen to John Douglas? Discuss with a partner.**

Sir Arthur Conan Doyle

1859

Sir Arthur Conan Doyle (born May 22, 1859, Edinburgh, Scotland—died July 7, 1930, Crowborough, England) was a Scottish writer, best known for his creation of the detective Sherlock Holmes, one of the most famous detectives in crime fiction.

A doctor, writer and believer in the supernatural, Conan Doyle's great imagination and scientific training contributed to the world of mystery and science fiction. He was a man of science but he also believed in fairies and the spirit world.

1881

His Early Life

Conan Doyle loved adventure and travel. To earn some money while he was studying medicine, he worked as a ship's doctor on short trips to Antarctic and Africa. Based on these experiences and the stories he loved as a child, he began to write short stories. He graduated from Edinburgh University with a medical degree at the age of 22. At that time, although he came from a very religious family, he turned away from religion and began to go to seances.

1916

Conan Doyle and Spiritualism

In 1916, Conan Doyle publicly declared he was a spiritualist. He believed that communication with spirits was possible, and wrote books, articles and made speeches about it. Conan Doyle was tricked by mediums, later proven to be dishonest, but he continued to believe in spiritualism, right up until his death.

And then there were the fairies...

He wrote a book in 1922 called *The Coming of the Fairies*, in which he defended the stories of two young girls who said they had photographed each other playing with real fairies. Long after Conan Doyle's death, they admitted to having used paper cut-outs for the fairies. Interestingly, Conan Doyle's own Uncle Richard had invented, in his book illustrations, the typical representation of a fairy as a little girl with wings, just like the ones in the photo.

An Important Figure

Conan Doyle was an important public and political figure. He was knighted for his volunteer work during the Boer War, and during the First World War, he worked for the Foreign Office. He even solved real-life mysteries, to free two unjustly imprisoned men.

An Inspiration to Others

His novel *The Lost World* was probably the inspiration for Jurassic Park and other films, and the 1932 film *The Mummy* was based on his story, "The Ring of Thoth". His 1883 medical article called "Life and Death in the Blood," describes the imaginary voyage of a microscopic observer through the human body, which was the main idea behind the film *Fantastic Voyage* in 1966.

First Novels

In 1886, Conan Doyle finished the first Sherlock Holmes novella, *A Study in Scarlet*. After several rejections, he sold it for £25 for inclusion in the 1887 Beeton's Christmas Annual. It was reprinted in 1889 and many more times, but he never earned another penny from it. *Sign of the Four*, the second book with Holmes and Watson, also had only a little success. While writing the early Holmes stories, Doyle also wrote novels based on British history, which he considered more important. Although greatly admired, none of these novels had the success of the Sherlock Holmes short stories that appeared in *The Strand Magazine*, starting in 1891. After writing three series of Holmes stories, which earned him a lot of money, Conan Doyle was tired of the popular detective and killed him off in the 1893 story, "The Final Problem." His readers reacted strongly to Holmes's death. They wrote letters to Conan Doyle, begging him to bring Holmes back. In 1902, he decided to publish his third Holmes novel, *The Hound of the Baskervilles*. It appeared in nine parts in *The Strand Magazine*, but was presented as an old case from before Holmes's death. Conan Doyle finally really brought Holmes back in 1903, in "The Empty House." He continued, reluctantly, to write Holmes stories until three years before his death.

Task Solve the anagrams.

Conan Doyle was a **RCOTOD** and writer and was best known for the creation of the famous **VTECIDETE** Sherlock Holmes. Many of these stories, which **ANDERE** him a lot of money, were published in the Strand **ZAGIMANE**. Originally from a religious family, he became a spiritualist and believed in the **LAPSUNUTERAR** and the existence of **IFERAIS**.

Sherlock Holmes

The classic description of Sherlock Holmes, everyone would agree, is of a tall thin man with a long, pointed nose, wearing a cape and a deerstalker hat and carrying a magnifying glass. He plays the violin, often smokes a pipe, and behaves in an eccentric manner. In reality, Holmes only wore that type of hat once in the original stories. His famous catchphrases are "Elementary, my dear Watson" and "Come Watson, the game is afoot!". True Sherlock fans will know that, in the Conan Doyle stories, Holmes never said "Elementary" to Dr Watson or anyone else.

Holmes in film and on TV

Over the years, the role of Sherlock Holmes has been played by many excellent actors and interpreted in different ways. From the earliest films with Basil Rathbone and Peter Cushing to later ones with Robert Downey Jr., and TV series from Jeremy Brett and Benedict Cumberbatch, who brought Holmes into the 21st century, to Jonny Lee Miller in Elementary, which took place in a modern-day New York City with a female Dr Watson. There have also been versions with young Sherlock and old Sherlock.

221b Baker Street, London

Fans of Sherlock Holmes will know that he lived in apartment B at 221 Baker Street in London. Now, visitors to London can visit his fictional home, which is now the Sherlock Holmes museum. When Conan Doyle introduced the residence in the novel A Study in Scarlet in 1887, this address did not even exist.

The numbers at that time actually stopped at no.85, and were only extended in the 1920s.

Dr John H. Watson

Dr Watson is Holmes' best friend, assistant and flatmate. He returned to London from Afghanistan, after working as a surgeon in the British Army, and met Holmes when he was looking for a place to stay. He is described as a classic Victorian gentleman, unlike the more eccentric Holmes. He is intelligent but not as good at solving mysteries as Holmes is.

Watson is the narrator of almost all of the Sherlock Holmes stories and first appeared in the novel A Study in Scarlet (1887).

At the end of the book, Watson is annoyed that Scotland Yard has taken credit for solving the Holmes' case and exclaims, 'Your merits should be publicly recognised. You should publish an account of the case. If you won't, I will for you'. Holmes suavely responds: 'You may do what you like, Doctor'. Therefore, the story is presented as 'a reprint from the reminiscences of John H. Watson'.

Task

How many different Sherlock Holmes films or TV series have you seen? Which Sherlock did you like best? Compare with a friend.

Test Yourself

Complete the sentences about the novel with A, B or C.

Part 1

1 Prof. Moriarty is a ...
   ☐ **A** doctor.   ☐ **B** teacher.   ☐ **C** mathematician.

2 The clues to the cipher were in...
   ☐ **A** a bible.   ☐ **B** an almanac.   ☐ **C** a dictionary.

3 Cecil Barker had first met John Douglas in ...
   ☐ **A** California.   ☐ **B** London.   ☐ **C** Birlstone.

4 Sherlock Holmes and Dr Watson were welcomed at Birlstone station by ...
   ☐ **A** Sergeant Wilson. ☐ **B** Inspector MacDonald. ☐ **C** White Mason.

5 On the dead man's arm there was the design of...
   ☐ **A** a triangle inside a circle. ☐ **B** a circle inside a triangle.

   ☐ **C** a circle inside a square.

6 Sherlock Holmes found the second dumb-bell ...
   ☐ **A** under the table   ☐ **B** behind the curtain   ☐ **C** in the moat.

Part 2

1 At the start of Chapter 1, McMurdo met Scanlan on the train.
   He said he lived in ...
   ☐ **A** Vermissa.   ☐ **B** Hobson's Patch.   ☐ **C** Chicago.

2 When Mr Shafter heard that McMurdo was a Freeman, he told him ...
   ☐ **A** to go to the lodge.   ☐ **B** to speak to Boss McGinty.
   ☐ **C** to find other lodgings.

3 As well as being the Bodymaster of the Lodge, McGinty was also ...
   ☐ **A** the town councillor.   ☐ **B** the head of the police.
   ☐ **C** a mine owner.

4 Mr Morris met McMurdo in the park ...
   ☐ **A** to tell him he was leaving Vermissa.
   ☐ **B** to warn him about the Scowrers.
   ☐ **C** to offer him a job in his shop.

5 Birdy Edwards was ...
   ☐ **A** a reporter.   ☐ **B** a Scowrer.   ☐ **C** a detective.

6 Ted Baldwin got out of prison ...
   ☐ **A** after 3 years.   ☐ **B** after 5 years.   ☐ **C** after 10 years.

Syllabus

Level B2
This reader contains the items listed below as well as those included in previous levels of the ELI Readers syllabus.

Topics
Crime/Mystery
Secret Societies
Mining Towns in 19th century America

Grammar
Present and Past Tenses
Present and Past Perfect Tenses
Modals of obligation, Modal auxiliaries, Modals of deduction
Passive forms
Gerunds
Zero, First, Second and Third Conditionals
Infinitive constructions
Relative pronouns
Direct and Indirect Speech
Phrasal verbs

Young Adult (ELI) Readers